SRA Imagine It!

**Level 3
Book 1**

Program Authors

Carl Bereiter

Andy Biemiller

Joe Campione

Iva Carruthers

Doug Fuchs

Lynn Fuchs

Steve Graham

Karen Harris

Jan Hirshberg

Anne McKeough

Peter Pannell

Michael Pressley

Marsha Roit

Marlene Scardamalia

Marcy Stein

Gerald H. Treadway Jr.

McGraw Hill SRA

Columbus, OH

Acknowledgments

Grateful acknowledgment is given to the following publishers and copyright owners for permissions granted to reprint selections from their publications. All possible care has been taken to trace ownership and secure permission for each selection included. In case of any errors or omissions, the Publisher will be pleased to make suitable acknowledgments in future editions.

FRIENDSHIP

"New Neighbors" from COULD WE BE FRIENDS? POEMS FOR PALS by Bobbi Katz. Copyright © 1997. Used by permission of Mondo Publishing.

"The Legend of Damon and Pythias" from THE BAG OF FIRE AND OTHER PLAYS by Fan Kissen. Copyright © 1964 by Houghton Mifflin Company, renewed © 1993 by John Kissen Heaslip. Reprinted by permission of Houghton Mifflin Company. All rights reserved. By permission of John Kissen Heaslip.

TEAMMATES by Peter Golenbock, text copyright © 1990 by Golenbock Communications, illustrations copyright © 1990 by Paul Bacon, reprinted by permission of Harcourt, Inc. This material may not be reproduced in any form or by any means without prior written permission of the publisher.

RUGBY & ROSIE by Nan Rossiter. Copyright © Nan Rossiter, 1997. Published by arrangement with Dutton Children's Books, a member of Penguin Group (USA) Inc.

Reprinted with permission of The National Geographic Society from GOOD-BYE, 382 SHIN DANG DONG by Frances Park and Ginger Park. Text copyright © 2002 Frances Park and Ginger Park. Illustrations copyright © 2002 Yangsook Choi.

"Since Hanna Moved Away" Reprinted with the permission of Atheneum Books for Young Readers, an imprint of Simon & Schuster Children's Publishing Division from IF I WERE IN CHARGE OF THE WORLD AND OTHER WORRIES by Judith Viorst. Text copyright © 1981 Judith Viorst.

SRAonline.com

 SRA

ANIMALS AND THEIR HABITATS

"I have no hatchet" from IF NOT FOR THE CAT by Jack Prelutsky, illustrated by Ted Rand. COPYRIGHT © 2004. Used by permission of HarperCollins Publishers.

From MAKE WAY FOR DUCKLINGS by Robert McCloskey, copyright 1941, renewed © 1969 by Robert McCloskey. All rights reserved including the right of reproduction in whole or in part in any form. This edition published by arrangement with Viking Children's Books, a member of Penguin Young Readers Group, a division of Penguin Group (USA) Inc.

"We are we are we…" from IF NOT FOR THE CAT by Jack Prelutsky, illustrated by Ted Rand. COPYRIGHT © 2004. Used by permission of HarperCollins Publishers.

"BEHIND THE REDWOOD CURTAIN" Text copyright © 2000 by Natasha Wing. Published as part of the anthology MY AMERICA: A POETRY ATLAS OF THE UNITED STATES by Simon and Schuster Children's Publishing. All rights reserved. Used with the permission of Sheldon Fogelman Agency, Inc.

TWO DAYS IN MAY by Harriet Peck Taylor, pictures by Leyla Torres. Copyright (c) 1999 by Harriet Peck Taylor, illustrations copyright © 1999 by Leyla Torres. Reprinted by permission of Farrar, Straus & Giroux, LLC.

From THE CRINKLEROOTS GUIDE TO KNOWING ANIMAL HABITATS by Jim Arnosky. Text and illustrations copyright © 1986 by Jim Arnosky. All rights reserved. Reprinted by arrangement with the Susan Schulman Agency.

WOLF ISLAND by Celia Godkin. Copyright © 1989 Celia Godkin. Used by permission of Fitzhenry and Whiteside.

ONE SMALL PLACE IN A TREE by Barbara Brenner, illustrated by Tom Leonard. Copyright © 2004. Used by permission of HarperCollins Publishers.

"Safe inside my pouch…" from IF NOT FOR THE CAT by Jack Prelutsky, illustrated by Ted Rand. COPYRIGHT © 2004. Used by permission of HarperCollins Publishers.

MONEY

"Lemonade Stand" reprinted with the permission of Margaret K. McElderry Books, an imprint of Simon & Schuster Children's Publishing Division from WORLDS I KNOW AND OTHER POEMS by Myra Cohn Livingston. Text copyright © 1985 Myra Cohn Livingston. From WORLDS I KNOW AND OTHER POEMS by Myra Cohn Livingston. Copyright © 1985 by Myra Cohn Livingston. Used by permission of Marian Reiner.

"Tony and the Quarter" from ROLLING HARVEY DOWN THE HILL TEXT COPYRIGHT © 1985 by Jack Prelutsky. Used by permission of HarperCollins Publishers.

From UNCLE JED'S BARBER SHOP. Text copyright © 1993 by Margaree King Mitchell. Illustrations copyright © 1993 by James Ransome. Reproduced by arrangement with Simon & Schuster Books for Young Readers, Simon & Schuster Children's Publishing Division. All rights reserved.

From MADAM C.J. WALKER: SELF-MADE MILLIONAIRE (Revised Edition) by Patricia and Frederick McKissack. Copyright © 2001 by Enslow Publishers, Inc., Berkeley Heights, NJ. All rights reserved.

From THE GO-AROUND DOLLAR by Barbara Johnston Adams, Illustrated by Joyce Audy Zarins. Text Copyright © 1992 by Barbara Johnston Adams. Illustrations Copyright © 1992 by Joyce Audy Zarins. Reprinted by arrangement with Simon & Schuster Books for Young Readers, an Imprint of Simon & Schuster Children's Publishing Division. All rights reserved.

"It's a Deal!" by Catherine Ripley. Reprinted by permission of Cricket Magazine Group, Carus publishing Company, from CLICK magazine, January 2001, Volume 4, Number 1, copyright, © 2000 by Catherine Ripley.

LEMONS AND LEMONADE by Nancy Loewen, illustrated by Brian Jensen. Copyright © 2004. Used with permission of Picture Window Books.

Program Authors

Carl Bereiter, Ph.D.
University of Toronto

Andy Biemiller, Ph.D.
University of Toronto

Joe Campione, Ph.D.
University of California, Berkeley

Iva Carruthers, Ph.D.
Northeastern Illinois University

Doug Fuchs, Ph.D.
Vanderbilt University

Lynn Fuchs, Ph.D.
Vanderbilt University

Steve Graham, Ed.D.
Vanderbilt University

Karen Harris, Ed.D.
Vanderbilt University

Jan Hirshberg, Ed.D.
Reading Specialist

Anne McKeough, Ph.D.
University of Toronto

Peter Pannell
Principal, Longfellow Elementary School,
Pasadena, California

Michael Pressley, Ph.D.
Michigan State University

Marsha Roit, Ed.D.
National Reading Consultant

Marlene Scardamalia, Ph.D.
University of Toronto

Marcy Stein, Ph.D.
University of Washington, Tacoma

Gerald H. Treadway Jr., Ed.D.
San Diego State University

Unit 1

Table of Contents

Friendship

Unit Overview.......................➤ 12

Vocabulary Warm-Up.....................➤ 14

Rugby & Rosie American Bookseller "Pick of the Lists" •

Golden Sower Award ·······················➤ 16

realistic fiction written and illustrated by Nan Parson Rossiter

Meet the Author/Illustrator, Nan Parson Rossiter ······➤ 34

Theme Connections························➤ 35

Social Studies Inquiry A Bright Idea ········➤ 36

Vocabulary Warm-Up.....................➤ 38

The Legend of Damon and Pythias.......................➤ 40

myth adapted as a play by Fan Kissen • illustrated by Christian Slade

Meet the Author, Fan Kissen

Meet the Illustrator, Christian Slade ···············➤ 58

Theme Connections························➤ 59

Social Studies Inquiry From Athens to America 60

Vocabulary Warm-Up ················➤ 62

Good-bye, 382 Shin Dang Dong

⁂ Award-winning authors ··············➤ 64

realistic fiction by Frances Park and Ginger Park • illustrated by Yangsook Choi

Meet the Authors, Frances Park and Ginger Park

Meet the Illustrator, Yangsook Choi ··············➤ 82

Theme Connections ··············➤ 83

🌐 Social Studies Inquiry Ellis Island—

Immigration Station ··············➤ 84

Vocabulary Warm-Up ··············➤ 86

Beauty and the Beast ··············➤ 88

fairy tale illustrated by John Palacios

Meet the Illustrator, John Palacios ··············➤ 104

Theme Connections ··············➤ 105

🌐 Social Studies Inquiry Outlook Is "Rosy" for City Parks
··············➤ 106

Vocabulary Warm-Up ··············➤ 108

Teammates ⁂ Notable Children's Trade Book (Social Studies) • Award-winning illustrator ··············➤ 110

biography by Peter Golenbock • illustrated by Paul Bacon

Meet the Author, Peter Golenbock

Meet the Illustrator, Paul Bacon ··············➤ 122

Theme Connections ··············➤ 123

🌐 Social Studies Inquiry Guiding the Way to Freedom
··············➤ 124

New Neighbors ··············➤ 126

a poem by Bobbi Katz • illustrated by Marion Eldridge

Since Hanna Moved Away ⁂ Notable

Children's Trade Book (Social Studies) • Award-winning illustrator ··········➤ 127

a poem by Judith Viorst • illustrated by Marion Eldridge

Test Prep ··············➤ 128

Animals and Their Habitats

Unit Overview ....➤ **132**

Vocabulary Warm-Up ....➤ **134**

One Small Place in a Tree

⭐ Outstanding Science Trade Book for Students K–12 Award ......➤ **136**

expository text by Barbara Brenner • *illustrated by* Tom Leonard

Meet the Author, Barbara Brenner

Meet the Illustrator, Tom Leonard ....➤ **154**

Theme Connections ....➤ **155**

Science Inquiry Please Feed the Birds ....➤ **156**

Vocabulary Warm-Up ....➤ **158**

Make Way for Ducklings

⭐ Caldecott Medal ....➤ **160**

fantasy written and illustrated by Robert McCloskey

Meet the Author/Illustrator, Robert McCloskey ....➤ **170**

Theme Connections ....➤ **171**

Science Inquiry Frozen Frogs ....➤ **172**

Vocabulary Warm-Up •••••••••••••••••••••••••► 174

Wolf Island ⭐ Children's Literature Roundtable of Canada
Information Book Award •••••••••••••••••••••••► 176
narrative nonfiction written and illustrated by Celia Godkin
Meet the Author/Illustrator, Celia Godkin •••••••••► 190
Theme Connections •••••••••••••••••••••••••► 191
🐾 **Science** **Inquiry** Ancient Wolves ••••••••••► 192

Vocabulary Warm-Up •••••••••••••••••••••► 194

Two Days in May
⭐ Parent's Choice Recommendation •••••••••••••► 196
realistic fiction by Harriet Peck Taylor • illustrated by Leyla Torres
Meet the Author, Harriet Peck Taylor
Meet the Illustrator, Leyla Torres •••••••••••► 212
Theme Connections •••••••••••••••••••••••► 213
🐾 **Science** **Inquiry** A National Pleasure ••••••► 214

Vocabulary Warm-Up •••••••••••••••••••••••► 216

**Crinkleroot's Guide to Animal
Habitats** ⭐ Award-winning author ••••••••••••► 218
narrative nonfiction written and illustrated by Jim Arnosky
Meet the Author/Illustrator, Jim Arnosky •••••••••► 240
Theme Connections •••••••••••••••••••••••••► 241
🐾 **Science** **Inquiry** Deserts Are Not Deserted •••► 242

Haiku poems from **If Not for the Cat** ⭐
Award-winning Poet • Award-winning illustrator ••••••••► 244
by Jack Prelutsky • illustrated by Ted Rand

Behind the Redwood Curtain ••••••► 246
poem by Natasha Wing • illustrated by Lori Anzalone

Test Prep •••••••••••••••••••••••► 248

Unit 3

Table of Contents

Money

Unit Overview . . . . ➤ 252

Vocabulary Warm-Up . . . . ➤ 254

It's a Deal! . . . . ➤ 256
from Click magazine
expository text by Catherine Ripley • *illustrated by* R. W. Alley

Meet the Author, Catherine Ripley

Meet the Illustrator, R. W. Alley . . . . ➤ 264

Theme Connections . . . . ➤ 265

Social Studies Inquiry Good as Gold . . . . ➤ 266

Vocabulary Warm-Up . . . . ➤ 268

The Go-Around Dollar . . . . ➤ 270
realistic fiction/expository text by Barbara Johnston Adams • *illustrated by* Joyce Audy Zarins

Meet the Author, Barbara Johnston Adams

Meet the Illustrator, Joyce Audy Zarins . . . . ➤ 292

Theme Connections . . . . ➤ 293

Social Studies Inquiry Children Cherish Chance to Learn
. . . . ➤ 294

Vocabulary Warm-Up · ➤ 296

Lemons and Lemonade: A Book about Supply and Demand · · · · · · · · · ➤ 298
narrative nonfiction by Nancy Loewen · *illustrated by* Brian Jensen

Meet the Author, Nancy Loewen

Meet the Illustrator, Brian Jensen · · · · · · · · · · · · · · · ➤ 310

Theme Connections · · · · · · · · · · · · · · · · · · · ➤ 311

Social Studies Inquiry Hooray for Hybrids · · · · ➤ 312

Vocabulary Warm-Up · ➤ 314

Madam C. J. Walker: Self-Made Millionaire
Carter G. Woodson Book Award, National Council of the Social Studies · · · ➤ 316
biography by Patricia and Fredrick McKissack

Meet the Authors, Patricia and Fredrick McKissack · · · · · · · · · · ➤ 326

Theme Connections · ➤ 327

Social Studies Inquiry An International Request · · ➤ 328

Vocabulary Warm-Up · ➤ 330

Uncle Jed's Barbershop ALA Notable
Children's Book · Coretta Scott King Honor Award for Illustration · · · · · · · · ➤ 332
historical fiction by Margaree King Mitchell · *illustrated by* James Ransome

Meet the Author, Margaree King Mitchell

Meet the Illustrator, James Ransome · · · · · · · · · · · · · · · · ➤ 344

Theme Connections · ➤ 345

Social Studies Inquiry The Great Depression · · · · · ➤ 346

Lemonade Stand Award-winning poet · · · · · · · · ➤ 348
poem by Myra Cohn Livingston · *illustrated by* Laura Freeman-Hines

Tony and the Quarter
Award-winning poet · ➤ 350
poem by Jack Prelutsky · *illustrated by* Erica Pelton Villnave

Test Prep · ➤ 352

Glossary · ➤ 356

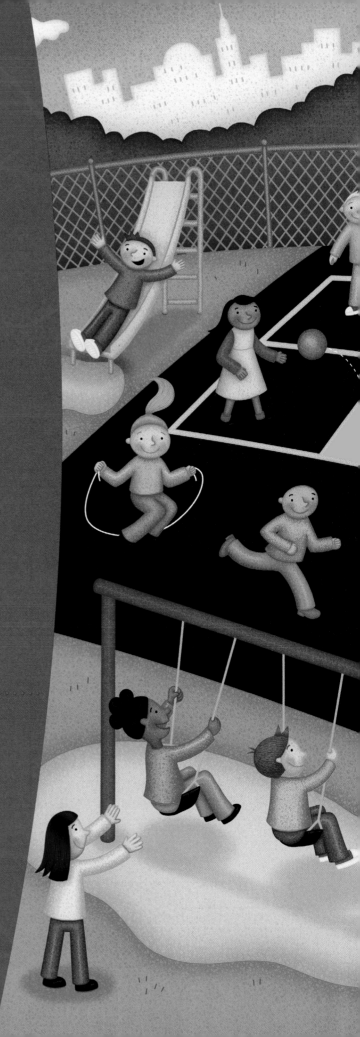

Unit 1

Friendship

Being a friend is always easy. Or is it? Sometimes it takes a lot of work to be a good friend. Sometimes you become friends with people whom you never thought you would. Having good friends can bring joy, fun, and happiness to our lives. Who is your best friend?

Theme Connection

Look at the illustration. What types of activities are the children doing? How are some children playing as friends? How else could the children be showing friendship to each other?

12

BIG Idea

What does it take to be a good friend?

13

Read the story to find the meanings of these words, which are also in "Rugby & Rosie":

✦ chores
✦ permission
✦ worried
✦ energy
✦ grateful
✦ patient
✦ especially
✦ ignore

Vocabulary Strategy

Context Clues are hints in the text. They help you find the meanings of words. Use context clues to find the meaning of *ignore*.

Vocabulary
Warm-Up

Jen cleared the table, finishing the last of her chores. It was time for fun! Jen wanted to go exploring in the woods with her dog, Pirate. Jen's house was surrounded by trees. As long as she stayed close by, Jen had permission to play in the woods with Pirate.

Jen called, "Pirate! Here, girl!" Pirate did not come. Jen was worried and went to search for her dog. At last, Jen heard a whimper in the garage.

Jen found Pirate curled up in a corner. Pirate licked Jen's hand, but the dog did not have the energy to stand up. Jen raced to get her parents. Her parents decided Pirate should see a doctor right away.

14

Jen's family was grateful, or thankful, that Dr. Boyd could see Pirate so soon. Sadly, he gave them bad news: Pirate had a virus. Dr. Boyd did not know if Pirate would get better. They would have to wait and see.

It was tough to be patient, especially for Jen. After six days, Pirate was still weak. Jen sat with the dog for hours each day. She tried hard to ignore how worried she felt.

One night, Jen checked on Pirate; the dog's bed was empty! Jen dashed to the backyard, nervous about what she might find. As she scanned the woods, Jen saw something move. It was Pirate! The dog had made her way to the woods, where she stood wagging her tail. Jen knew then that her brave dog was going to be okay.

GAME

Synonyms

On a sheet of paper, make a list of the vocabulary words you found in this story. Beside each word, write a synonym for that word. When you and a classmate are both finished, compare the synonyms you listed for each vocabulary word.

Concept Vocabulary

The concept word for this lesson is *affection.* **Affection** is a friendly feeling of liking or loving. There is often great affection between pets and the people who take care of them. Talk about ways that pets and people show their affections for one another.

RUGBY & Rosie

by Nan Parson Rossiter

Focus Questions

What is it like to have a
pet as a best friend? What
would it be like to lose a
friend, even if it were for
a good reason?

17

Rugby is my dog. He is a chocolate Labrador,
and we have had him for as long as I can
remember.

He walks with me to the school-bus stop in
the morning, and he meets me there when I
get home. He follows me around when I do my
chores, and he sleeps beside my bed at night.
He is my best friend.

We used to do everything together—just the
two of us.

Then Rosie came.

One fall day, my dad brought home a little yellow puppy. Her name was Rosie. She was so cute that I loved her right away. But she wasn't an ordinary puppy. She was coming to live with my family for only a year.

Then Rosie would be old enough to go to a special school. There she would learn how to be a guide dog for a blind person. She and her new owner would always be together. They would be best friends. Just like Rugby and me.

I knew all this before Rosie came, but Rugby didn't. I held the puppy out to him to see how he would greet Rosie. She leaned forward eagerly and licked Rugby right on the nose.

Rugby gave one sniff and turned away. He made it very clear he wasn't interested in being friends.

"Come on, Rugby," I said. "She wants to play with you." And it was true. Rosie did want to play. But Rugby wasn't in the mood.

My mom and dad told me to be patient with Rugby, that he'd get used to having another dog around the house. But I wasn't sure. He looked so sad. Maybe he thought I didn't love him anymore, which wasn't true!

Rosie fit in with the family right away. She was so friendly and always wanted to play. She would chase after anything and then run back. She loved everyone in the family—even Rugby! But he still wasn't friendly. Day after day, Rugby just moped around and wouldn't play with us.

That didn't bother Rosie one bit. She thought Rugby was the greatest. She trotted along after him, ran between his legs, tripped him, jumped on him, and barked at him.

Rugby did his best to ignore her.

But Rosie just wouldn't give up.

Then one day, Rugby was not waiting at the
school-bus stop. I was worried. He *always* met me at
the bus stop.

I ran home—and there I found Rugby asleep on
the porch. Curled up in a little ball next to him was
Rosie. "Rugby!" I said. They both looked up at me
and wagged their tails. Rosie yawned and stretched
and settled back down against Rugby's side.

From then on, Rugby and Rosie were always together. They romped and played and chased the falling leaves. And they both waited for me at the bus stop.

Rosie was getting bigger. But she was still a puppy with lots of energy. Poor old Rugby tried his best to keep up! Soon winter came, and the three of us were racing and chasing through the new snow. We had so much fun together!

Sometimes it felt as if Rosie had always been with us—and always would be. I didn't want to think about the day when she would have to leave.

Rosie was old enough now for short lessons. Dad showed me how to teach her simple commands: *come, sit, stand, down, stay,* and *heel.*

We all worked to teach her good manners. A dog who begged for food at the table or jumped up on people would not make a good guide dog.

Rosie learned fast. Dad said that she was very smart and loved to please people. But she would have to pass many tests before she could become a guide dog.

I asked Dad what would happen if Rosie didn't pass the tests. He said that she couldn't be a guide dog, but she could still be a good pet. Then we would be able to keep her.

Now I didn't know what to think. I wanted Rosie to do well. I wanted to be proud of her. And I wanted her to help a blind person someday. I knew how important that was. But it was getting harder and harder to think of Rosie going away. And how could I explain it to Rugby? He loved Rosie as much as I did. Now the three of us were best friends.

When spring came, my family started taking Rosie on trips. We wanted her to be used to cars and buses and to the places where she would have to take her blind owner, like the bank and the store. We even took her to a restaurant. Of course, Rugby couldn't come with us. He always looked a little sad when Rosie got to go somewhere he couldn't go. And I knew he would be waiting for us when we got home.

Rosie would jump out of the car, and the two of them would race off, barking and playing and jumping. Later, they would come home in time for dinner, muddy and wet, with their tongues hanging out.

Soon summer came. The days were long and hot. Rosie was almost full grown. She was a beautiful dog. She and Rugby liked to sleep in the cool shade together. Sometimes the three of us went swimming in a nearby pond. Rugby and Rosie loved to fetch sticks and tennis balls that I threw into the water.

It was a wonderful summer, and I wanted it to last forever.

I knew that when fall came, it would be time for Rosie to go. When that day did come, I tried to be brave. Rugby and I stood and watched as Dad opened the car door for Rosie to jump in. Rugby wasn't upset. He didn't know that Rosie wasn't coming back. But I was so sad. I took Rugby on a long walk and tried not to think about Rosie. It was just like old times, before she came—when there were just the two of us.

When Dad came home, Rugby was waiting, his tail wagging. But, of course, Rosie wasn't in the car. Rugby looked all over for her. He whined. I wanted to explain everything, but I knew he couldn't understand. Instead, I buried my face in his neck and whispered, "She's gone, and I miss her, too."

We all missed Rosie very much, especially Rugby. Her trainers called several times. At first, I hoped that Rosie wasn't doing well. Then she could come back to live with us. But the trainers said that she was doing fine and would graduate with her new owner soon. That made me feel so mixed-up. I didn't want to think about Rosie with a new owner, but I knew how important Rosie would be to a person who needed her. Could that person love her as much as Rugby and I had?

I wanted to go to the graduation and see Rosie again. Then I had a great idea. I asked Dad if we could take Rugby, too. I knew how he'd missed Rosie—after all, they'd been best friends.

We got special permission for Rugby to go to the graduation. I could hardly wait.

At the graduation, there were lots of people and dogs. Rugby spotted Rosie right away. She was in her guide-dog harness, standing beside her new owner. She seemed so calm, and we thought she looked so proud. Rugby bounded over to her, pulling me along. The two dogs greeted each other nose to nose, tails wagging. But Rosie would not leave her owner's side. She was a working dog now with an important job to do.

Her owner talked to us for a while. She told us
how grateful she was to have Rosie and what a
wonderful dog she was. And she thanked us for
taking good care of her while she was a puppy.

When it was time to go, we said good-bye to
Rosie. Poor Rugby. On the way home in the car, I
tried to make him feel better. I talked to him and
patted him. I told him that her new owner loved
her and would take good care of her.

The next morning, Rugby was still moping around when my dad left in the car. I was excited— and nervous, too.

I knew where my dad was going.

When the car came back, I was waiting with Rugby. Dad got out. He had a wiggly little puppy in his arms. I knew I was holding on to Rugby too tightly—wishing, hoping. I wanted him to know that, because we had all loved Rosie so much, we had decided we would help raise another puppy that would be ours for a year.

Dad knelt down in front of Rugby. "Rugby," he said, "this is Blue."

And Rugby leaned forward and licked that little puppy right on the nose.

Nan Parson Rossiter

Nan Parson Rossiter has always loved to draw. After high school, she became a student at the Rhode Island School of Design. In 1991, she began writing her first children's book. It was based on experiences of a friend who was raising a guide dog. She now cares for a special dog named Chloe, a breeding dog for guide dogs. Rossiter lives in Connecticut, where she loves spending time with her husband and two sons, hiking and feeding the birds.

Theme Connections

Within the Selection

1. Rugby and the boy are best friends. What happened to the boy's friendship with Rugby when Rosie came to live with them?

2. Why did the boy in the selection sometimes wish that Rosie was not doing well with her trainers?

Beyond the Selection

3. Why can it be difficult sometimes to have a friendship with someone?

4. Do you have a pet that is your best friend? If so, what do you do together as friends?

Write about It!

Describe your friendship with a pet.

Be sure to look for pictures of people and their pets to add to the **Concept/ Question Board.**

A Bright Idea

Some people who are blind use tools to help them as they travel. Some get help from a guide dog or a person who can see. Others read Braille signs and menus with their fingers.

Another aid for those who are blind is the white cane. It is more than a tool. It is a symbol of independence too. The white cane is honored each year on October 15. This is "White Cane Safety Day."

George Bonham is the man who thought of the white cane. One day he saw a man who was blind waiting to cross a busy street. Bonham saw that the man held a black cane. The dark color blended in with the road. Drivers seemed to ignore the man.

This gave Bonham an idea. He knew that these canes helped people know what was in front of them as they walked. The cane helped them detect things such

Some traffic lights have a beeping signal. It tells people when it is safe to begin crossing the street.

as curbs, stairs, or other people. However, Bonham thought white canes would be more helpful. A white cane would be easy for drivers to see.

Bonham was part of a group called the Lions Club. He told them about his plan, and the group liked it. In 1930 the club began to provide white canes for people who are blind.

Soon, states started to pass "white cane laws." The laws help protect people who are blind. They tell how much room drivers should give a visually impaired person who is crossing the street. The laws say that drivers must be patient.

White cane laws have one more purpose. They support the rights of people who are blind. This includes the right to travel freely. The laws help those who are blind be active in their communities at school, work, and home.

Think Link

1. What does the caption tell you about crossing signals?

2. How did George Bonham behave like a responsible citizen?

3. What is the purpose of white cane laws?

Try It!

As you work on your investigation, think about how you can use pictures and captions in your final presentation.

Read the story to find the meanings of these words, which are also in "The Legend of Damon and Pythias":

- ✦ condition
- ✦ exchange
- ✦ deserted
- ✦ persuaded
- ✦ curious
- ✦ faith
- ✦ struggled
- ✦ miserable

Vocabulary Strategy

Apposition is when a word or group of words define another word in the same sentence. Use apposition to find the meaning of *exchange*.

Vocabulary
Warm-Up

Greek legends are full of kings and heroes. One of these was King Minos from the island of Crete. Minos was known to rule with strength and fairness.

One of the king's sons was a great athlete. He won many events at a sports contest in Athens. The king of Athens was jealous. He killed Minos's son. Minos was angry. He could have destroyed Athens, but he spared the city on one condition.

Minos forced the king of Athens to make an exchange, or trade, of citizens for his dead son. Athens had to send seven young men and women to Crete every nine years. In Crete, the young people were deserted in a labyrinth, or maze. In the

maze lived a fierce beast called the Minotaur. Those who entered were certain to die.

The king of Athens also had a son. His name was Theseus. One day the son persuaded the king to send him to Crete. Theseus was curious about the beast. He also had faith that he could kill it.

Theseus went to the palace in Crete. He was thrown in the maze, where he struggled with the Minotaur. Theseus prevailed! The beast was killed.

Theseus sailed home. He was supposed to fly a white flag to send a signal that he was alive, but he forgot. When the king of Athens did not see the white flag, he thought his son was dead. The miserable king leapt into the sea and died.

GAME

Flash Cards

Make a set of flash cards with the vocabulary words. Write the vocabulary word on one side of the card and its definition on the other side. Use the flash cards to review the vocabulary words and definitions. Then ask a classmate to use the cards to quiz you.

Concept Vocabulary

The concept word for this lesson is *sacrifice.* A **sacrifice** is something a person gives up for the sake of someone else. For example, Theseus was willing to sacrifice his safety to save others from the monster in Crete. Talk about how making a sacrifice for someone else makes you feel. How does it feel when someone makes a sacrifice for you?

Genre

A **play** tells a story by showing what the characters say and do. A play is written to be performed.

Comprehension Strategy

 Adjusting Reading Speed

As you read, you may find that some sentences are harder to read than others. Slow down or reread sections that you do not understand.

Focus Questions

What would be a true test of friendship? What would you be willing to give up for a friend?

40

The LEGEND
of Damon and Pythias

a myth adapted as a play by Fan Kissen

illustrated by Christian Slade

CAST

Damon	Second Voice
Pythias	Third Voice
Soldier	Announcer
King	Narrator
Mother	
First Robber	SOUNDS
Second Robber	*Iron door open and shut*
First Voice	*Key in lock*

ANNOUNCER: Hello, listeners! It's story time again. Today's story is about the strong friendship between two men. Listen, and you'll hear how one of these men was ready to give up his life for his friend's sake.

MUSIC: *(Up full and out)*

NARRATOR: Long, long ago there lived on the island of Sicily two young men named Damon and Pythias. They were known far and wide for the strong friendship each had for the other. Their names have come down to our own times to mean true friendship. You may hear it said of two persons:

FIRST VOICE: Those two? Why, they're like Damon and Pythias!

NARRATOR: The King of that country was a cruel tyrant. He made cruel laws, and he showed no mercy toward anyone who broke his laws. Now, you might very well wonder:

SECOND VOICE: Why didn't the people rebel?

NARRATOR: Well, the people didn't dare rebel, because they feared the King's great and powerful army. No one dared say a word against the King or his laws—except Damon and Pythias. One day a soldier overheard Pythias speaking against a new law the King had proclaimed.

SOLDIER: Ho, there! Who are you, that dares to speak so about our King?

PYTHIAS: *(Unafraid)* I am called Pythias.

SOLDIER: Don't you know it is a crime to speak against the King or his laws? You are under arrest! Come and tell this opinion of yours to the King's face!

MUSIC: *(A few short bars in and out)*

NARRATOR: When Pythias was brought before the King, he showed no fear. He stood straight and quiet before the throne.

KING: *(Hard, cruel)* So, Pythias! They tell me you do not approve of the laws I make.

PYTHIAS: I am not alone, your Majesty, in thinking your laws are cruel. But you rule the people with such an iron hand that they dare not complain.

KING: *(Angry)* But *you* have the daring to complain *for* them! Have they appointed you their champion?

PYTHIAS: No, your Majesty. I speak for myself alone. I have no wish to make trouble for anyone. But I am not afraid to tell you that the people are suffering under your rule. They want to have a voice in making the laws for themselves. You do not allow them to speak up for themselves.

KING: In other words, you are calling me a tyrant! Well, you shall learn for yourself how a tyrant treats a rebel! Soldier! Throw this man into prison!

SOLDIER: At once, your Majesty! Don't try to resist, Pythias!

PYTHIAS: I know better than to try to resist a soldier of the King! And for how long am I to remain in prison, your Majesty, merely for speaking out for the people?

KING: *(Cruel)* Not for very long, Pythias. Two weeks from today at noon, you shall be put to death in the public square, as an example to anyone else who may dare to question my laws or acts. Off to prison with him, soldier!

MUSIC: *(In briefly and out)*

NARRATOR: When Damon heard that his friend Pythias had been thrown into prison, and the severe punishment that was to follow, he was heartbroken. He rushed to the prison and persuaded the guard to let him speak to his friend.

DAMON: Oh, Pythias! How terrible to find you here! I wish I could do something to save you!

PYTHIAS: Nothing can save me, Damon, my dear friend. I am prepared to die. But there is one thought that troubles me greatly.

DAMON: What is it? I will do anything to help you.

PYTHIAS: I'm worried about what will happen to my mother and my sister when I'm gone.

DAMON: I'll take care of them, Pythias, as if they were my own mother and sister.

PYTHIAS: Thank you, Damon. I have money to leave them. But there are other things I must arrange. If only I could go to see them before I die! But they live two days' journey from here, you know.

47

DAMON: I'll go to the King and beg him to give you your freedom for a few days. You'll give your word to return at the end of that time. Everyone in Sicily knows you for a man who has never broken his word.

PYTHIAS: Do you believe for one moment that the King would let me leave this prison, no matter how good my word may have been all my life?

DAMON: I'll tell him that I shall take your place in this prison cell. I'll tell him that if you do not return by the appointed day, he may kill me, in your place!

PYTHIAS: No, no, Damon! You must not do such a foolish thing! I cannot—I will not—let you do this! Damon! Damon! Don't go! (To himself) Damon, my friend! You may find yourself in a cell beside me!

MUSIC: (In briefly and out)

DAMON: *(Begging)* Your Majesty! I beg of you! Let Pythias go home for a few days to bid farewell to his mother and sister. He gives his word that he will return at your appointed time. Everyone knows that his word can be trusted.

KING: In ordinary business affairs—perhaps. But he is now a man under sentence of death. To free him even for a few days would strain his honesty— *any* man's honesty—too far. Pythias would never return here! I consider him a traitor, but I'm certain he's no fool.

DAMON: Your Majesty! I will take his place in the prison until he comes back. If he does not return, then you may take *my* life in his place.

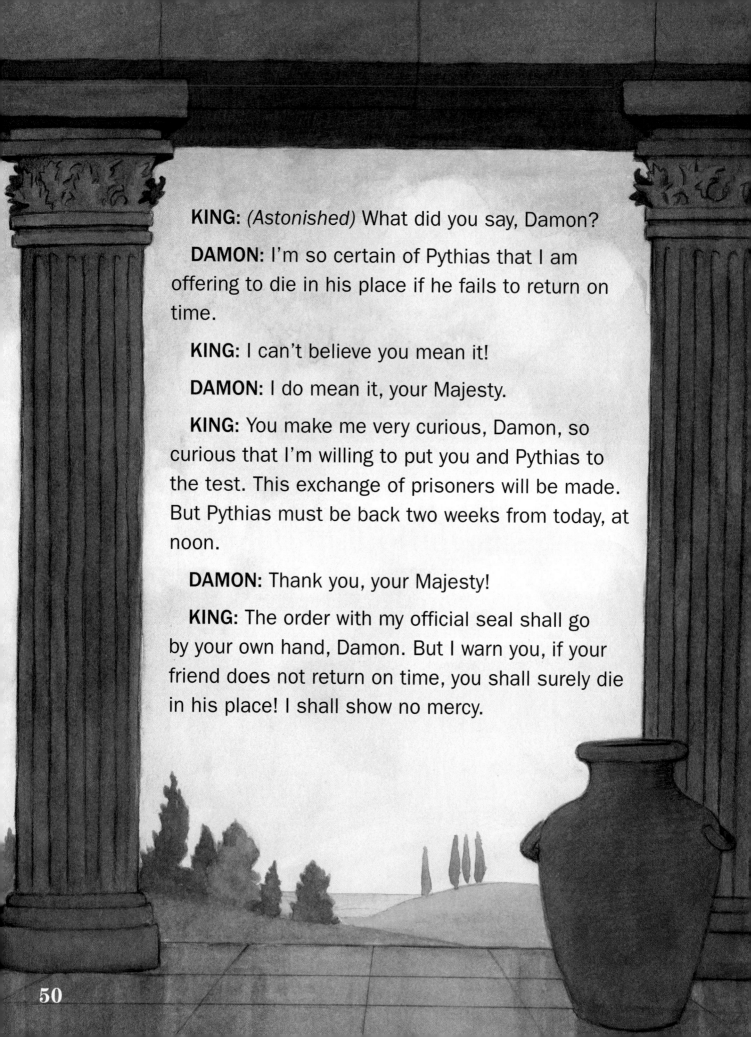

KING: *(Astonished)* What did you say, Damon?

DAMON: I'm so certain of Pythias that I am offering to die in his place if he fails to return on time.

KING: I can't believe you mean it!

DAMON: I do mean it, your Majesty.

KING: You make me very curious, Damon, so curious that I'm willing to put you and Pythias to the test. This exchange of prisoners will be made. But Pythias must be back two weeks from today, at noon.

DAMON: Thank you, your Majesty!

KING: The order with my official seal shall go by your own hand, Damon. But I warn you, if your friend does not return on time, you shall surely die in his place! I shall show no mercy.

MUSIC: (*In briefly and out*)

NARRATOR: Pythias did not like the King's bargain with Damon. He did not like to leave his friend in prison, with the chance that he might lose his life if something went wrong. But at last Damon persuaded him to leave, and Pythias set out for his home. More than a week went by. The day set for the death sentence drew near. Pythias did not return. Everyone in the city knew of the condition on which the King had permitted Pythias to go home. Everywhere people met, the talk was sure to turn to the two friends.

FIRST VOICE: Do you suppose Pythias will come back?

SECOND VOICE: Why should he stick his head under the King's axe, once he's escaped?

THIRD VOICE: Still, would an honorable man like Pythias let such a good friend die for him?

FIRST VOICE: There's no telling what a man will do when it's a question of his own life against another's.

SECOND VOICE: But if Pythias doesn't come back before the time is up, he will be killing his friend.

THIRD VOICE: Well, there's still a few days' time. I, for one, am certain that Pythias *will* return in time.

SECOND VOICE: And *I* am just as certain that he will *not*. Friendship is friendship, but a man's own life is something stronger, *I* say!

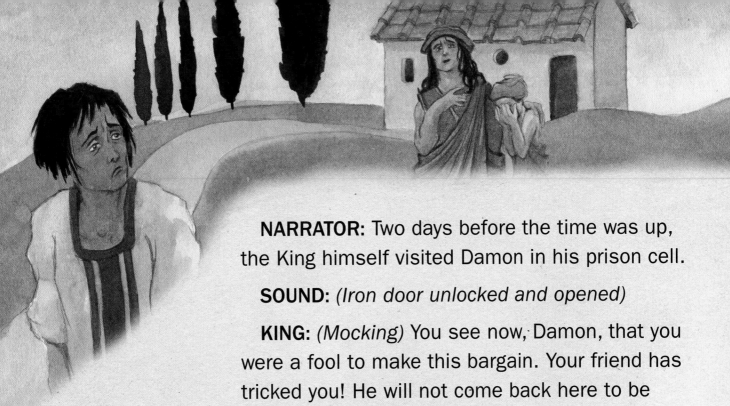

NARRATOR: Two days before the time was up, the King himself visited Damon in his prison cell.

SOUND: *(Iron door unlocked and opened)*

KING: *(Mocking)* You see now, Damon, that you were a fool to make this bargain. Your friend has tricked you! He will not come back here to be killed! He has deserted you.

DAMON: *(Calm and firm)* I have faith in my friend. I know he will return.

KING: *(Mocking)* We shall see!

SOUND: *(Iron door shut and locked)*

NARRATOR: Meanwhile, when Pythias reached the home of his family he arranged his business affairs so that his mother and sister would be able to live comfortably for the rest of their years. Then he said a last farewell to them before starting back to the city.

MOTHER: *(In tears)* Pythias, it will take you only two days to get back. Stay another day, I beg you!

PYTHIAS: I dare not stay longer, Mother. Remember, Damon is locked up in my prison cell while I'm gone. Please don't make it any harder for me! Farewell! Don't weep for me. My death may help to bring better days for all our people.

NARRATOR: So Pythias began his journey in plenty of time. But bad luck struck him on the very first day. At twilight, as he walked along a lonely stretch of woodland, a rough voice called:

FIRST ROBBER: Not so fast there, young man! Stop!

PYTHIAS: *(Startled)* Oh! What is it? What do you want?

SECOND ROBBER: Your money bags.

PYTHIAS: My money bags? I have only this small bag of coins. I shall need them for some favors, perhaps, before I die.

FIRST ROBBER: What do you mean, before you die? We don't mean to kill you, only take your money.

PYTHIAS: I'll give you my money, only don't delay me any longer. I am to die by the King's order three days from now. If I don't return to prison on time, my friend must die in my place.

FIRST ROBBER: A likely story! What man would be fool enough to go back to prison, ready to die.

SECOND ROBBER: And what man would be fool enough to die *for* you?

54

FIRST ROBBER: We'll take your money, all right. And we'll tie you up while we get away.

PYTHIAS: *(Begging)* No! No! I must get back to free my friend! *(Fade)* I must go back!

NARRATOR: But the two robbers took Pythias's money, tied him to a tree, and went off as fast as they could. Pythias struggled to free himself. He cried out for help as loud as he could, for a long time. But no one traveled through that lonesome woodland after dark. The sun had been up for many hours before he finally managed to free himself from the ropes that had tied him to the tree. He lay on the ground, hardly able to breathe.

MUSIC: *(In briefly and out)*

NARRATOR: After a while Pythias got to his feet. Weak and dizzy from hunger and thirst and his struggle to free himself, he set off again. Day and night he traveled without stopping, desperately trying to reach the city in time to save Damon's life.

MUSIC: *(Up and out)*

NARRATOR: On the last day, half an hour before noon, Damon's hands were tied behind his back and he was taken into the public square. The people muttered angrily as Damon was led in by the jailer. Then the King entered and seated himself on a high platform.

SOUND: *(Crowd voices in and hold under single voices)*

SOLDIER: *(Loud)* Long live the King!

FIRST VOICE: *(Low)* The longer he lives, the more miserable our lives will be!

KING: *(Loud, mocking)* Well, Damon, your lifetime is nearly up. Where is your good friend Pythias now?

DAMON: *(Firm)* I have faith in my friend. If he has not returned, I'm certain it is through no fault of his own.

KING: *(Mocking)* The sun is almost overhead. The shadow is almost at the noon mark. And still your friend has not returned to give you back your life!

DAMON: *(Quiet)* I am ready, and happy, to die in his place.

KING: *(Harsh)* And you shall, Damon! Jailer, lead the prisoner to the—

SOUND: *(Crowd voices up to a roar, then under)*

FIRST VOICE: *(Over noise)* Look! It's Pythias!

SECOND VOICE: *(Over noise)* Pythias has come back!

PYTHIAS: *(Breathless)* Let me through! Damon!

DAMON: Pythias!

PYTHIAS: Thank the gods I'm not too late!

DAMON: *(Quiet, sincere)* I would have died for you gladly, my friend.

CROWD VOICES: *(Loud, demanding)* Set them free! Set them both free!

KING: *(Loud)* People of the city! *(Crowd voices out)* Never in all my life have I seen such faith and friendship, such loyalty between men. There are many among you who call me harsh and cruel. But I cannot kill *any* man who proves such strong and true friendship for another. Damon and Pythias, I set you both free. *(Roar of approval from crowd)* I am King. I command a great army. I have stores of gold and precious jewels. But I would give all my money and power for one friend like Damon or Pythias.

SOUND: *(Roar of approval from crowd up briefly and out)*

MUSIC: *(Up and out)*

Meet the Author

Fan Kissen

Kissen wrote plays in a unique style. She wrote them as though they were radio shows, with announcers, sound effects, and background music. Kissen often wrote about folktales and legends in her plays. She also wrote an award-winning radio series called "Tales from the Four Winds." Kissen loved to travel. She visited many countries and spoke three languages.

Meet the Illustrator

Christian Slade

When he was young, Christian Slade carried a sketchbook with him wherever he went. He still does. Slade loves to draw—especially people, dogs, and robots. He has many things in his studio to give him ideas for drawings including comic books and his collections of toys and action figures. Slade lives in Florida with his wife Ann and their two Welsh corgi dogs, Penny and Leo.

Friendship
Theme Connections

Within the Selection

1. How did Damon show his friendship for Pythias?

2. How did the friendship of Damon and Pythias save their lives?

Across Selections

3. How is friendship in this story like friendship in "Rugby & Rosie"?

4. What other stories have you read that are about someone who makes a big sacrifice for a friend?

Beyond the Selection

5. What does "The Legend of Damon and Pythias" tell you about friendship?

6. Have you ever had to make a big sacrifice for a friend?

Write about It!

Describe a time when a friend made a big sacrifice for you.

Be sure to find articles about people making sacrifices for their friends to add to the **Concept/Question Board.**

Social Studies Inquiry

FROM ATHENS TO AMERICA

Athens, Greece, was the first known democracy in the world. The Greek word for it was *demokratia*. This means "the rule of the people." Our country is based on and has faith in this form of rule.

In a democracy, citizens take part in the government. In Athens, only free men over age 20 were allowed to be citizens. They could make speeches and vote. Women and slaves could not do these things.

Our democracy is not like that. Each person born here is a citizen. Both men and women over age 18 can vote.

The men of Athens would meet at an Assembly. They talked about rules they wanted to make or change. Each citizen had the right to speak there.

Our Congress is like the Assembly. Laws and rules are made in Congress. However, most citizens do not speak there. Instead, we vote for leaders who speak for us.

Athens had a court system. There were no judges or lawyers like we have now.

Each person stated his own case to a jury.

We still have juries. They, too, vote at the end of a trial. If they vote to *convict,* the person is found guilty. If they vote to *acquit,* the person is found innocent.

A jury might have to decide how a person who broke the law will pay for the crime. Maybe a fine will be set. Sometimes a person must go to jail.

For thousands of years, groups of people have set up rules to live by. While the rules may change, the need for them remains. It was true in ancient Greece, and it is true today.

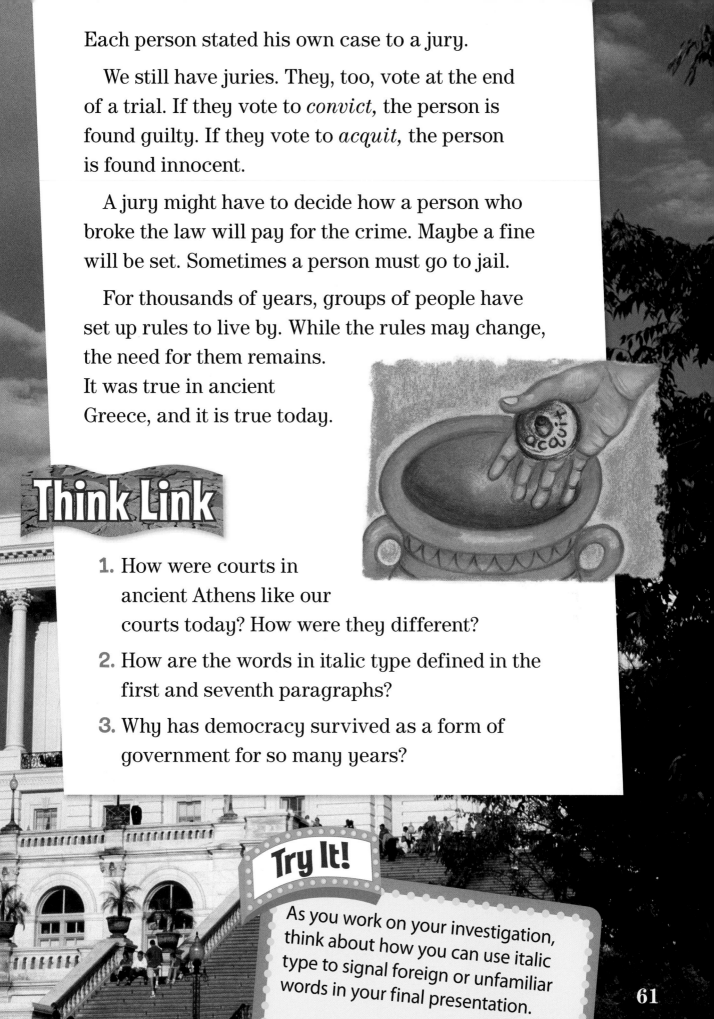

Think Link

1. How were courts in ancient Athens like our courts today? How were they different?

2. How are the words in italic type defined in the first and seventh paragraphs?

3. Why has democracy survived as a form of government for so many years?

Try It!

As you work on your investigation, think about how you can use italic type to signal foreign or unfamiliar words in your final presentation.

Genre

Realistic Fiction involves stories about people and events that are true to life and that could really happen.

Comprehension Skill

⭐ **Author's Point of View** As you read, identify whether the story is written in the first-person, second-person, or third-person point of view.

Good-bye,
382 Shin Dang Dong

by Frances Park and Ginger Park
Illustrated by Yangsook Choi

Focus Questions
How might you feel if you moved away from a close friend? If you moved to a new country, how would you make friends if you did not speak the same language as the people in your new neighborhood or school?

64   65

Read the article to find the meanings of these words, which are also in "Good-bye, 382 Shin Dang Dong":

✦ enthusiastic
✦ insisted
✦ foreign
✦ translation
✦ peculiar
✦ pastel
✦ glum
✦ assure

Vocabulary Strategy

Context Clues are hints in the text. They help you find the meanings of words. Use context clues to find the meaning of *glum*.

Vocabulary
Warm-Up

Do you like to get mail? Are you an enthusiastic writer? Then you might like to be a pen pal!

In the past, few schools insisted that students take part in pen pal programs. Now, many schools think having a pen pal is a great learning tool. It helps improve writing skills. It is also a good way to learn about a new culture.

Maybe you would like to have a pen pal from another country. This can help you practice a foreign language. Translation can be tricky, though. Be sure to check what you write! You do not want to insult your pen pal by mistake.

Foreign pen pals can help you start or add to a stamp collection. Compare stamps from around the

world. Save ones that are pretty and ones that are peculiar, or unusual. Gather stamps in a range of colors, from soft, pastel tones to bright hues.

One of the best parts of having a pen pal is making a new friend. Share your thoughts, whether you feel happy or glum. When your pen pal shares his or her feelings, try to assure him or her that you care.

Use your best manners when writing. This includes being tidy. A letter that is crumpled or streaked with ink is hard to read.

Remember, writing is not a chore. It should be fun! So, find a cushion and get comfortable. Put your thoughts on paper, and send them off to a friend.

GAME

Charades

Use the vocabulary words to play a game of charades with classmates. Choose one of the words to act out. The first person to correctly identify the word and explain its meaning will take the next turn as actor.

Concept Vocabulary

The concept word for this lesson is **thoughtfulness. Thoughtfulness** is showing concern for others and their feelings. What are some examples of thoughtfulness that you have witnessed or have been part of? How can thoughtfulness lead to friendship? Discuss your ideas with classmates.

Genre

Realistic Fiction involves stories about people and events that are true to life and that could really happen.

Comprehension Skill

 Author's Point of View

As you read, identify whether the story is written in the first-person, second-person, or third-person point of view.

Good-bye, 382 Shin Dang Dong

by Frances Park and Ginger Park
illustrated by Yangsook Choi

Focus Questions

How might you feel if you moved away from a close friend? If you moved to a new country, how would you make friends if you did not speak the same language as the people in your new neighborhood or school?

My heart beats in two places: Here, where I live,
and also in a place where I once lived. You see, I was
born in Korea. One day my parents told me we were
moving to America. I was eight years old, old enough
to keep many lovely memories of my birthplace alive
in my heart forever. But one very sad memory stays
with me, too. The day I cried, "Good-bye, 382 Shin
Dang Dong!"

On that summer day I woke up to the sound of light
rain tapping on my window. The monsoon season was
coming. I didn't even need to open my eyes to know
that. It was that time of year. It was also time to move.

In a few hours, I would be on an airplane.

When I opened my eyes, my heart sank. My bedroom was so bare! No hand-painted scrolls or colorful fans on my walls. No silk cushions or straw mats on my floor. All my possessions were packed away in a big brown box marked "Lovely Things."

I frowned and listened to the raindrops. One, two, three . . . Soon the thick of the monsoon would arrive, and a thousand raindrops would hit our clay-tiled roof all at once. But I wouldn't be here to listen to them. I would be halfway around the world in a strange, foreign place called 112 Foster Terrace, Brighton, Massachusetts, U.S.A.

My parents were very excited.

"Jangmi, you will like America," Dad tried to assure me.

"Are the seasons the same?" I wondered.

"Oh, yes."

"With monsoon rains."

"No, Jangmi, no monsoon rains."

"No friends either," I moaned.

"You will make many new friends in America," Mom promised me, "in your new home."

But I loved my home right here! I didn't want to go to America and make new friends. I didn't want to leave my best friend, Kisuni.

After breakfast, Kisuni and I ran out in the rain and to the open market. Monsoon season was also the season for sweet, yellow melons called *chummy*. Kisuni and I would often peel and eat chummy under the willow tree that stood outside my bedroom window. But today, the chummy were for guests who were coming over for a farewell lunch.

At the market we peered into endless baskets and took our time choosing the ripest, plumpest chummy we could find.

"Do they have chummy in America?" Kisuni wondered.

"No," I replied. "But my mom says they have melons called honeydew."

"Honeydew," Kisuni giggled. "What a funny name!"

Soon after we returned, family
and friends began to arrive,
carrying pots and plates of food.
One by one they took off their shoes,
then entered the house. Grandmother
was dressed in her most special occasion *hanbok*.
She set up the long *bap sang* and before I could
even blink, on it were a big pot of dumpling soup
and the prettiest pastel rice cakes I had ever seen.
Kisuni and I peeled and sliced our chummy and
carefully arranged the pieces on a plate.

Then everybody ate and sang traditional Korean
songs and celebrated in a sad way. Love and
laughter and tears rippled through our house. How
I wanted to pack these moments into a big brown
box and bring them with me to America.

70

Kisuni and I sneaked outside and sat beneath the willow tree. We watched the rain with glum faces.

"Kisuni, I wish we never had to move from this spot," I said.

"Me, too," she sighed. "Jangmi, how far away is America?"

"My mom says that it's halfway around the world. And my dad told me that when the moon is shining here, the sun is shining there. That's how far apart we'll be," I moaned.

"That's really far," Kisuni moaned back.

We watched the rain and grew more glum than ever. Then Kisuni perked up.

"So when you're awake, I'll be asleep. And when I'm awake, you'll be asleep," she declared. "At least we'll always know what the other one is doing."

That moment our faces brightened. But a moment later we had to say good-bye.

Kisuni held back her tears. "Promise you'll write to me, Jangmi."

"I promise, Kisuni."

It was time to go to the airport.

"Kimpo Airport," Dad instructed the taxi driver.

The taxi slowly pulled away. I looked at our beautiful home one last time. Like rain on the window, tears streaked down my face.

"Good-bye, 382 Shin Dang Dong!" I cried.

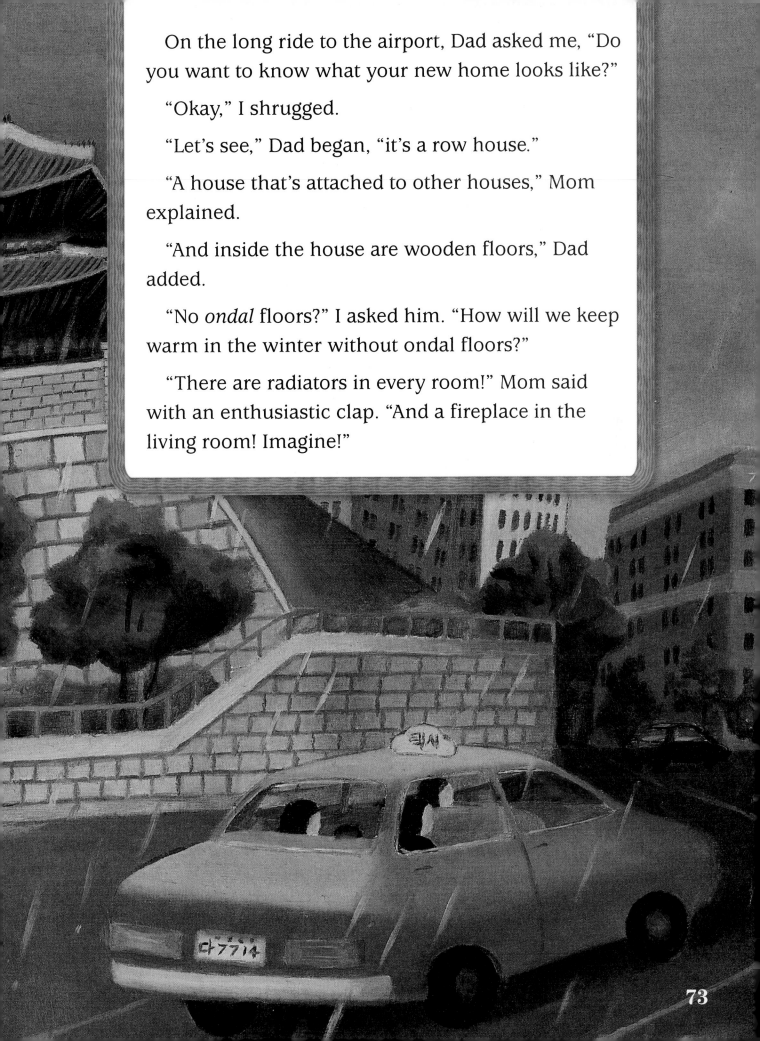

On the long ride to the airport, Dad asked me, "Do you want to know what your new home looks like?"

"Okay," I shrugged.

"Let's see," Dad began, "it's a row house."

"A house that's attached to other houses," Mom explained.

"And inside the house are wooden floors," Dad added.

"No *ondal* floors?" I asked him. "How will we keep warm in the winter without ondal floors?"

"There are radiators in every room!" Mom said with an enthusiastic clap. "And a fireplace in the living room! Imagine!"

73

No, I could not imagine that. In our home we had a fire in the cellar called the ondal. It stayed lit all the time. The heat from the ondal traveled through underground pipes and kept our wax-covered floors warm and cozy. A fireplace in the living room sounded peculiar to me.

"And the rooms are separated by wooden doors," Mom added.

"No rice paper doors?" I wondered.

My parents shook their heads. "No, Jangmi."

My eyes closed with disappointment. I had a hard time picturing this house. Would it ever feel like home?

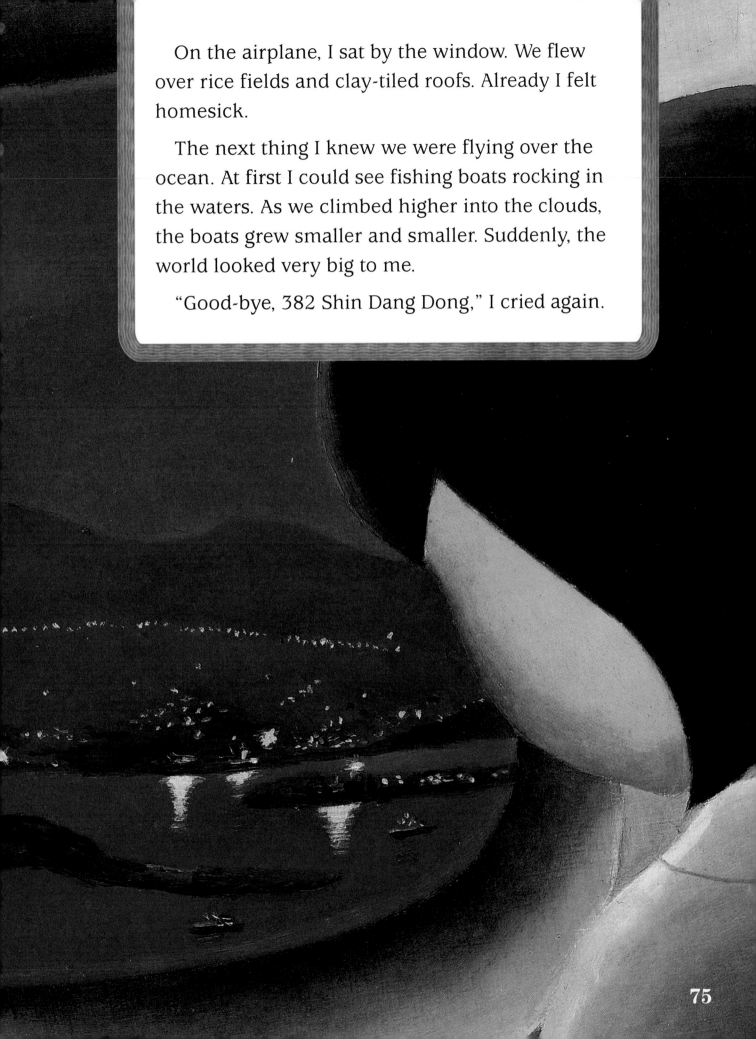

On the airplane, I sat by the window. We flew over rice fields and clay-tiled roofs. Already I felt homesick.

The next thing I knew we were flying over the ocean. At first I could see fishing boats rocking in the waters. As we climbed higher into the clouds, the boats grew smaller and smaller. Suddenly, the world looked very big to me.

"Good-bye, 382 Shin Dang Dong," I cried again.

Dad sat back in his seat and began to read an American newspaper. The words were all foreign.

"Dad," I asked, "how will I ever learn to understand English?"

"It's not so hard," he said. "Would you like to learn an English word?"

"Okay," I sighed.

After a pause, Dad came up with—

"Rose."

"Rose?" I repeated. "What does that mean?"

"That's the English translation of your Korean name," Mom said.

"Rose means Jangmi?" I asked.

"Yes," my parents nodded.

"Rose," I said over and over.

"Would you like to adopt Rose as your American name?" Mom asked me.

"No, I like *my* name," I insisted.

On a foggy morning four days later, we arrived in Massachusetts. After we gathered our luggage, we climbed into an airport taxi.

Even through the fog, I could see that things were very different in America. There were big, wide roads called highways. The rooftops were shingled instead of clay-tiled. People shopped in glass-enclosed stores instead of open markets. No rice fields, no monsoon rains. So many foreign faces.

Slowly, the taxi pulled up to a row house on a quiet street. Red brick steps led up to a wooden door.

"Here we are, Jangmi," Dad said, "112 Foster Terrace, Brighton, Massachusetts, U.S.A."

The house was just as my parents had described. I took off my shoes and walked on wooden floors. They felt very cold. I opened wooden doors. They felt very heavy. Outside, the fog had lifted. But inside, everything felt dark and strange.

"Look," Dad pointed out the window, "there's a tree just like the one at home."

"No, it's not, Dad. It's not a willow tree," I said.

"No," he agreed. "It's a maple tree. But isn't it beautiful?"

382 Shin Dang Dong, 382 Shin Dang Dong. I wanted to go home to 382 Shin Dang Dong right now. Only a knock at the door saved me from tears.

Mom announced, "The movers are here!"

The house quickly filled up with furniture and big brown boxes. The box marked "Lovely Things" was the last to arrive.

I unpacked all my possessions. I hung my hand-painted scrolls and colorful fans on the walls. I placed my silk cushions and straw mats on the floor.

Then came another knock. To our surprise a parade of neighbors waltzed in carrying plates of curious food. There were pink-and-white iced cakes and warm pans containing something called casseroles.

A girl my age wandered up to me with a small glass bowl. Inside the bowl were colorful balls. They smelled fruity.

She pointed to a red ball and said, "Watermelon!" She pointed to an orange ball and said, "Cantaloupe!" Lastly she pointed to a green ball and said, "Honeydew!"

I took a green ball and tasted it. Mmm . . . it was as sweet and delicious as chummy.

The girl asked me a question. But I couldn't understand her.

"She wants to know what kind of fruit you eat in Korea," Dad stepped in.

"Chummy," I replied.

"Chummy," the girl repeated, then giggled—just like Kisuni!

She asked me another question.

"She wants to know your name," Dad said.

Maybe someday I would adopt Rose as my American name. But not today.

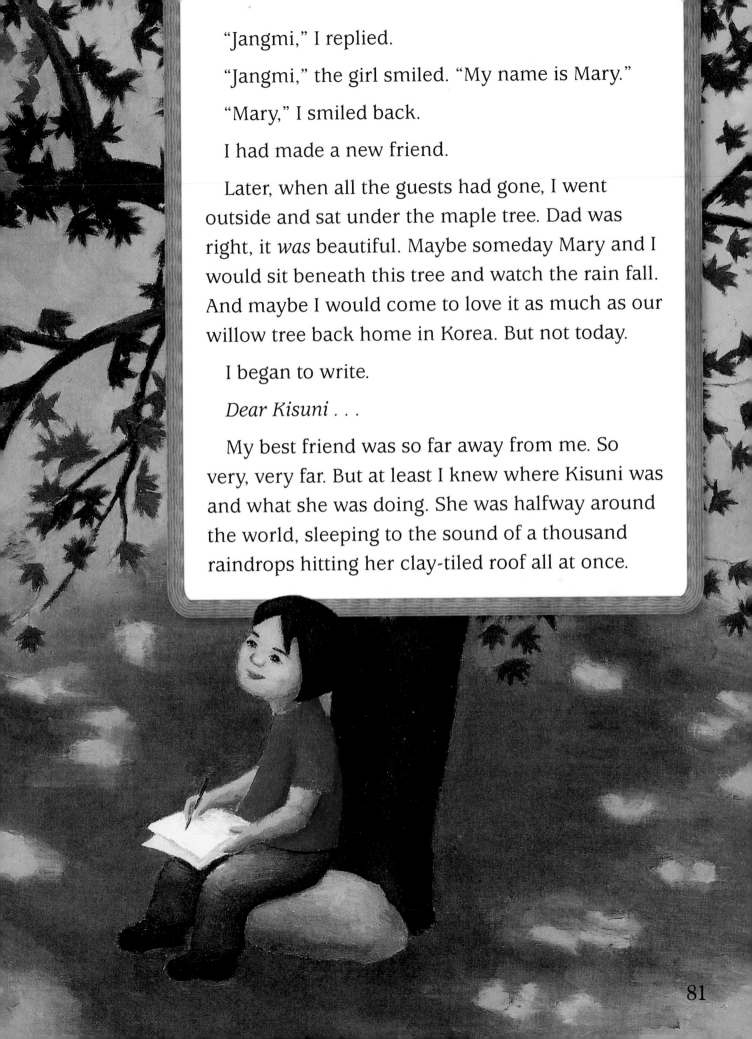

"Jangmi," I replied.

"Jangmi," the girl smiled. "My name is Mary."

"Mary," I smiled back.

I had made a new friend.

Later, when all the guests had gone, I went outside and sat under the maple tree. Dad was right, it *was* beautiful. Maybe someday Mary and I would sit beneath this tree and watch the rain fall. And maybe I would come to love it as much as our willow tree back home in Korea. But not today.

I began to write.

Dear Kisuni . . .

My best friend was so far away from me. So very, very far. But at least I knew where Kisuni was and what she was doing. She was halfway around the world, sleeping to the sound of a thousand raindrops hitting her clay-tiled roof all at once.

Meet the Authors

Frances Park and Ginger Park

Frances Park and Ginger Park are sisters. They write novels together and also own a business—a shop called Chocolate Chocolate in Washington, D.C. The Park sisters' parents moved from Korea to the D.C. area over fifty years ago. The sisters' stories often blend their parents' lives with their own American upbringing.

Meet the Illustrator

Yangsook Choi

Yangsook Choi was named Yangsook because *yang* means "sweet and nice," and *sook* means "clean and pure." Choi picked an American name, Rachel, when she and her family moved to America from Seoul, Korea. She still uses both names. Choi says being a child at heart helps her be a better writer and illustrator.

Friendship
Theme Connections

Within the Selection

1. What do you think Jangmi is going to miss most about Korea?

2. How did the family's new neighbors show friendship toward them?

Across Selections

3. How is friendship in this story like friendship in "Rugby & Rosie"?

4. What other stories have you read that are about someone who must leave his or her best friend?

Beyond the Selection

5. How can a long-distance friendship be made stronger?

6. What are some ways you can make new friends?

Write about It!

Describe a time when you made a new friend.

Remember to write down questions about making new friends to add to the **Concept/Question Board.**

Ellis Island— Immigration Station

Dear Park Director:

I would like to thank you and your enthusiastic staff for a job well done. You made my trip to Ellis Island so special. I was thrilled to see where my ancestors began their life in America.

Your staff helped me find James Doyle in the passenger records. He was my great, great grandpa. I even got to see a picture of the ship he sailed on!

I know that James Doyle was just one of millions of immigrants who came through Ellis Island. Like most of them, he left his home to search for a better life. Ellis Island was thought of as the "golden door" to that life.

The tour guide helped me understand what James went through on the long journey. Two weeks in the dark, stuffy bottom of a ship sounds awful. I am sure he missed his home in Ireland. He must have wondered about the choice he had made.

I could also imagine his joy, however. I learned that as the ship neared the Port of New York, passengers rushed up to the deck. From there, they could see the Statue of Liberty! She stood tall as a symbol of freedom and hope.

I was moved to learn about Ellis Island. I am also glad to know of my own link to that historic place. I will not forget the great tour and your staff's kindness. Thank you again.

Yours truly,
Patrick Doyle

Think Link

1. Did the writer choose an appropriate closing for this letter? Explain your answer.

2. Why was Ellis Island thought of as the "golden door"?

3. What did the writer learn about his great, great grandfather's journey?

Ellis Island
Immigration Museum

Try It!

As you work on your investigation, remember to include a closing in any letter you might need to write for research.

Read the story to find the meanings of these words, which are also in "Beauty and the Beast":

+ despair
+ mercy
+ sighed
+ timidly
+ clung
+ flattered
+ splendor
+ magnificent

Vocabulary Strategy

Word Structure is when parts of a word help you understand the word's meaning. Use word structure to find the meaning of *timidly*.

Vocabulary
Warm-Up

Trey read the poster by his classroom door. It said that the school was putting on a musical, "The Shoemaker and the Elves." All students were invited to try out for a part.

Trey knew the old tale. He liked the story of how a poor man's kindness is rewarded. Trey also had a great voice, but he was quite shy. He did not know if he could sing in front of other people. Still, he thought he might give it a shot.

At the audition, the students trying out for a part drew numbers. Trey had the misfortune of drawing number 1. He would sing first.

Trey was in despair. He searched the room for someone who might have mercy and trade numbers with him.

TRYOUTS THIS FRIDAY
THE SHOEMAKER
AND THE ELVES
THE MUSICAL
EVERYONE IS WELCOME!

But it was too late. The music teacher called out, "Number 1, please!"

Trey sighed as he timidly stepped onto the stage. He knew his song by heart, but still he clung to the sheet music. Trey took a deep breath and started singing.

He poured his heart into the song. It seemed that Trey actually became the simple shoemaker, too poor to pay his debts. Trey captured the character's grief at the prospect of losing his business.

When Trey finished the song, the room exploded with cheers. Trey was flattered with praise by students and teachers alike. He stood, stunned, and soaked up the splendor of the moment.

At last, Trey made his way to a seat. He had done it! Trey smiled as he thought to himself, "There's nothing magnificent about that shoemaker's life. Even so, it felt pretty good to be him."

Write a Riddle

Make up a riddle for each of the vocabulary words. For example, for the word *despair,* you might write, "Hope, you see, is the opposite of me." Exchange papers with a classmate and solve each other's riddles.

Concept Vocabulary

The concept word for this lesson is *kindness.* **Kindness** is showing gentle and caring behavior toward others. Often, one act of kindness leads to another. Why is this so? Record your ideas in a journal.

Beauty and the Beast

illustrated by John Palacios

Focus Questions

What is it like to watch a friendship grow deeper over time? How have you become friends with someone you did not like at first?

Once upon a time there lived a very rich merchant who had three sons and three daughters. The girls were all beautiful, but the youngest was so lovely that she was called Beauty. This made her sisters very jealous.

Beauty was not only prettier than her sisters, but she was also smarter than they were. And unlike them, she was both helpful and kind. The sisters hated her for her kind heart and laughed at her because she spent her time reading good books instead of going to parties and balls as they did.

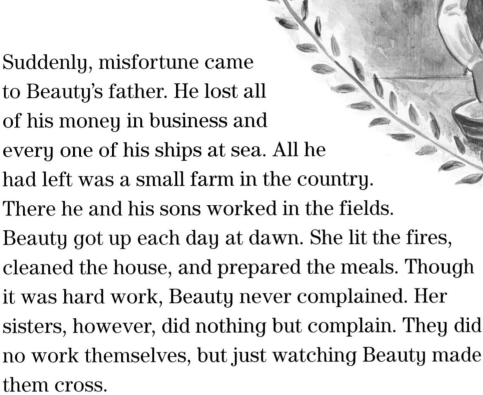

Suddenly, misfortune came
to Beauty's father. He lost all
of his money in business and
every one of his ships at sea. All he
had left was a small farm in the country.
There he and his sons worked in the fields.
Beauty got up each day at dawn. She lit the fires,
cleaned the house, and prepared the meals. Though
it was hard work, Beauty never complained. Her
sisters, however, did nothing but complain. They did
no work themselves, but just watching Beauty made
them cross.

After a year, news came that one of their father's
ships had not been lost but, filled to the top with
riches, had sailed safely into port. Before their
father left to meet the ship, the older sisters asked
him to bring back some jewels and dresses for
them. Beauty did not ask for anything.

"What shall I bring for you, Beauty?" her father asked.

"The only wish I have is to see you come home safely," she answered.

"But surely there is something you would like to have," said her father.

"Well, dear Father, then bring me a rose," said Beauty. "I love roses very much, and I have not seen one for a very long time."

In town, the merchant used most of the money from the ship's cargo to pay old debts. He started home as poor as when he had left. Deep snow and bitter frost made it impossible for his horse to carry him home that evening.

Night fell, and wolves were howling all around him. The merchant had lost his way in the deep forest, when suddenly he saw lights shining among the trees. When he hurried closer, he saw a magnificent castle standing in a beautiful park. He went through the open gate, got off his horse, and entered the castle. He saw nobody and heard not a sound.

The merchant sat down in
front of a friendly fire, where a
delicious dinner was waiting for him.
He ate the dinner with much pleasure
and hoped that he could soon thank his good
host, but nobody appeared. He fell asleep
after his meal and did not wake up until late
the next morning. Next to him he saw a fine
new suit in place of his old one.

"A kind fairy must own this castle," the
merchant thought, but he did not see or
hear any sign of life in the whole palace.
Finally he went down into the lovely
garden, where birds were singing
and flowers were blooming. The
beautiful roses reminded him
of Beauty's wish, and he
picked one of them.

Just then he heard a terrible roar, and
a frightful Beast rushed up. It seemed to be
very angry and said in a terrible voice, "Why are
you stealing my roses? Did I not shelter you in my
palace? Is this the way you say thank you? For
this I shall kill you!"

The merchant was terrified. He threw himself
on his knees and begged for mercy.

"I meant no harm, Your Majesty. I took the rose
for one of my daughters. She asked me to bring
her one. Please forgive me, Your Majesty."

"My name is not Majesty," roared the creature.
"My name is Beast. I do not like to be flattered.
Go home to your daughters. Ask whether one of
them is willing to die for you. If they refuse, you
must return yourself."

The merchant turned pale at the thought, but he promised to come back. He thought, I'll go and say farewell to my family. He found his horse already saddled, and soon he was home. He gave Beauty the rose and said, "Beauty, here is your rose. I had to pay a high price for it."

Then he told his daughters all that had happened. The older daughters wept loudly and begged their father not to go back. But Beauty said, "You have to keep your promise to the Beast, and I will go with you, dear Father."

But her father shook his head, "I will not let you go. I will go alone. I am old, and I shall die soon anyway."

Beauty stood firm. "Father, I *must* go," she said. "I would die of grief if I caused your death."

So Beauty said good-bye to her sisters and brothers and bravely mounted the horse with her father. Soon they reached the palace. In the dining hall they found a table set for two with golden plates, crystal glasses, and delicious food. They sat down to eat. Beauty thought, the Beast wants to fatten me up so that I will taste better when he eats me.

After dinner they heard the Beast's footsteps coming closer and closer. Beauty trembled and clung to her father. The Beast entered with a loud roar. Beauty was certain that he would eat her, but she tried to hide her fear and greeted him politely.

"Did you come willingly?" asked the Beast in his terrible voice.

"Yes," answered Beauty.

"You are very good. I
am pleased with you," said
the Beast. "Your father must leave
tomorrow, and he can never come back.
Good night, Beauty."

"Good night, Beast," she said.

Beauty went to bed, and as she slept that night,
she saw a beautiful fairy in her dreams. The fairy
said, "Beauty, you have a good heart, and you
shall be rewarded."

After her father had left the next morning,
Beauty wept. She thought that the Beast would
surely eat her this very night. Bravely she tried
not to worry. "I'll enjoy my last day
and explore the palace," she said
to herself. She walked through
many rooms. She found each
one more brilliant than
the last, until finally she
came to a door marked
Beauty's Apartment.

She opened the door timidly, and
there she saw the room of her dreams.
There were shelves of books, a piano, music,
beautiful needlework for her to do, and everything
else she could wish for. That night, as she sat down
to supper, she heard the Beast coming. She began
to tremble, for she wondered if he meant to eat
her now.

The Beast only said gruffly, "Good evening,
Beauty," and sat down and kept her company
during the dinner.

"Everything here is yours," he said after a while.
"Your wish is law. I hope that you will be happy
here. I am only a stupid Beast. Tell me, do you find
me very ugly?"

"Yes," said Beauty. "I cannot lie, but I think you
are also very good and kind and not stupid at all."

Beauty had almost forgotten to be afraid of the monster when he asked her, "Do you love me, Beauty? Will you marry me?"

Beauty was silent. At last she said honestly, "No, Beast, I cannot marry you."

The Beast sighed deeply and then left the room.

Three months passed. Beauty had everything she could wish for. She had become used to the ugliness of the Beast. She even looked forward to the evenings, when he always came to talk to her. He was so good and kind that she liked him more and more.

Every night he asked her to marry him. One night Beauty said, "Beast, you are my best friend, and you are very dear to me, but I don't think I shall ever be able to marry you."

"Beauty," said the Beast, "I will die without you. Please promise that you will never leave me." Beauty became very sad. She was very homesick for her father and longed to see him once more. She begged the Beast to let her go.

"Please let me go home for a week, Beast. We are good friends, and I promise to come back."

"Very well. I cannot let you suffer," said the Beast. "But if you are not back in one week, your faithful Beast will die. When you are ready to come back, you have only to turn your ring on your finger." And the Beast sighed even more loudly than usual.

The next morning when Beauty woke up, she was in her father's house. She dressed in the gold and diamond gown that the kind Beast had sent, and she went to greet her father. How happy the merchant was when he saw his daughter! He hugged and kissed her and laughed and cried for joy all at the same time.

Beauty's brothers had joined the army, but her sisters, who were married now and who lived close by, came to see her. They were not at all happy to see Beauty dressed like a queen, looking lovelier than ever before. In their jealousy they planned to keep her longer than seven days so that she would break her promise to the Beast.

"Perhaps then he will eat her," they said. They treated Beauty so well and put on such a show of kindness that Beauty agreed to stay another week.

On the tenth night, Beauty dreamed that the Beast was lying on the grass in his garden, dying of despair. "Oh, my poor Beast," she cried. "He cannot help being ugly. He has a good and kind heart, and that is worth more than anything."

She turned her ring on her finger and at once found herself back in her beautiful palace. She looked everywhere for her Beast. Then she remembered her dream, and she ran into the garden. There lay the Beast, quite still.

"What if I have killed him?" thought Beauty, terrified.

Beauty forgot the Beast's ugliness and bent over him. His heart was still beating faintly. Suddenly he opened his eyes. He whispered to her, "I cannot live without you. Now that you are here, I will die happy."

"No, Beast, you cannot die," cried Beauty. "I never knew how much I loved you until now. I was afraid that I was too late to save your life. I cannot live without you, dear Beast. Let me be your wife."

As Beauty spoke these words, a blaze of light sprang up through the whole palace. Music filled the air. Suddenly the Beast disappeared, and in his place stood a handsome prince.

"Where is my Beast?" cried Beauty.

"I am he," answered the prince. "I was turned into a Beast by a powerful witch. Only a beautiful girl who could love me for my kind heart could break the spell. Only you could help me, for you love goodness more than beauty and riches. Please, Beauty, be my queen."

Beauty gave the prince her hand, and he led her into the castle. There Beauty found her father and all her family. The fairy who had appeared in Beauty's dream had brought them all there. What joy and happiness!

"Beauty," said the fairy, "you will be a great queen. You will find beauty, wisdom, and goodness in the prince, who loves you. This is the reward for your good heart."

Beauty and her prince were married in great splendor, and they lived happily ever after.

Meet the Illustrator

John Palacios

When he was younger, John Palacios loved comic books. Now he works as an artist and spends a lot of time reading. Palacios enjoys drawing people. He likes to show how people might feel when they are in a special place. In a story, a special place might be fun, scary, or made-up. When Palacios draws a character in one of these settings, he feels like he is in the story too.

Friendship

Theme Connections

Within the Selection

1. Why did Beauty go to the castle with her father?
2. How was Beauty rewarded for her kindness to the Beast?

Across Selections

3. How is friendship in this story like friendship in "The Legend of Damon and Pythias"?
4. What other stories have you read that are about someone who sees the inner beauty in others?

Beyond the Selection

5. What does "Beauty and the Beast" tell you about friendship?
6. How can you show kindness to someone who has a hard time making friends?

Write about It!

Describe someone you know who sees the inner beauty in others.

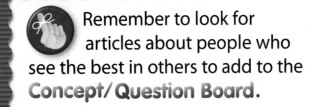

Remember to look for articles about people who see the best in others to add to the **Concept/Question Board.**

Outlook Is "Rosy" for City Parks

Last night's City Council meeting was of special interest to Megan Lee. Lee is director of the Park of Roses. She clung to her seat as votes for the proposed "Rose Rule" were read aloud. The new law would make it a crime to pick flowers at a public park. The law passed by a vote of 10 to 0.

"I'm so glad to see that kind of support for the law," said Lee. "It seems like common sense that you shouldn't take flowers from a park. I guess some people felt they had a right to the roses anyway. Now they know they don't. The flowers are there for all of us to enjoy."

Last June, Lee went to the head of the Parks Board. At that time, she expressed her wish to preserve the park's splendor. Lee had noticed that blooms had been clipped from quite a few plants. She asked if a law could be passed to deter guests from taking the flowers.

The Parks Board agreed to take the issue to Council; Council Member Juan Hill said he would sponsor the bill. As with all new laws, the "Rose Rule" was presented at three City Council meetings. This gave citizens a chance to speak out about the proposed law. Two people opposed it. Both felt that, because they pay city taxes, they should have a right to use the parks as they wish.

Clearly, Council did not agree. All votes were in favor of the law, which the mayor said she, too, will approve. After the law is signed, anyone caught taking a flower from a park will be fined.

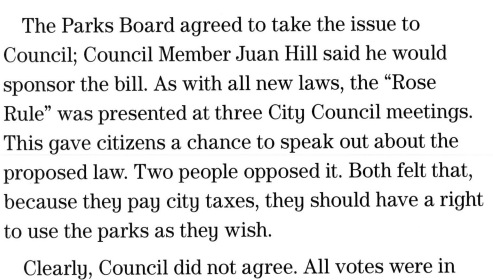

Think Link

1. Why did Megan Lee think the "Rose Rule" was necessary?

2. Why are proposed laws presented at three City Council meetings?

3. What does the quote in paragraph 2 contribute to the news story?

Try It!

As you work on your investigation, think about how you can use quotes to make your final presentation more interesting.

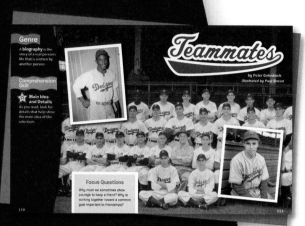

Genre
A **biography** is the story of a real person's life that is written by another person.

Comprehension Skill

★ **Main Idea and Details**
As you read, look for details that help show the main idea of the selection.

Teammates
by Peter Golenbock
illustrated by Paul Bacon

Focus Questions
Why must we sometimes show courage to keep a friend? Why is working together toward a common goal important to friendships?

110   111

Read the article to find the meanings of these words, which are also in "Teammates":

+ responded
+ leagues
+ compete
+ series
+ possess
+ opponents
+ challenge
+ equal

Vocabulary Strategy

Apposition is when a word or group of words define another word in the same sentence. Use apposition to find the meaning of *leagues*.

Vocabulary
Warm-Up

Soccer is popular with kids of all ages. Many people like the fast pace of the sport. Now, more kids than ever have a chance to play the game.

As more kids grew to like soccer, schools and other organizations took action. They responded by creating teams and leagues, which are groups of teams. Some towns have quite a few leagues for kids.

Many community centers have soccer leagues. They try to find an open position on a team for all kids who want to play. In this kind of league, teams from the same area compete against each other.

In some leagues the teams travel to other towns. Kids try out for these teams. Coaches put the kids through a series of drills. They watch for kids who possess speed and skill.

It takes more than skill to be a great athlete, though. It is also important to be a good sport. This means you treat others the way you would like to be treated. You show respect for your opponents. You do not want to challenge the referee's calls.

The spread of soccer has given numerous kids the chance to be part of a team. All players on a team have different skills. Even so, each team member can play as an equal.

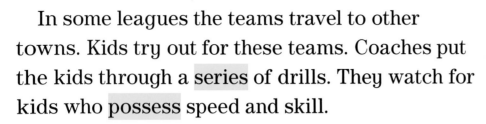

Crossword Puzzle

Create a crossword puzzle with the vocabulary words. First, decide how you will have the words overlap. Then draw empty boxes for the letters. Create separate sets of clues for words that go "Across" and words that go "Down." Give your puzzle to a classmate to complete.

Concept Vocabulary

The concept term for this lesson is *peer pressure.* Peers are people who are the same age or in the same group. **Peer pressure** is when one or more members of the group try to influence another person in the group. The person feels pressure to act a certain way. Think of some ways peer pressure can have a positive influence. Then think of some ways it can have a negative influence. Talk about your ideas.

Meet the Author

Peter Golenbock

Peter Golenbock is a famous sports writer whose books have been best sellers. He started writing, in part, because of his love for baseball. Golenbock has also been a sports-radio, talk-show host and a broadcaster for baseball. He and his wife and son live in St. Petersburg, Florida.

Meet the Illustrator

Paul Bacon

Paul Bacon has many interests, including writing, drawing cartoons, and photography. Bacon is known as being both funny and well-traveled. He has lived in eighteen cities, including two in Japan. He has also traveled to more than thirty countries, from Australia to Uzbekistan.

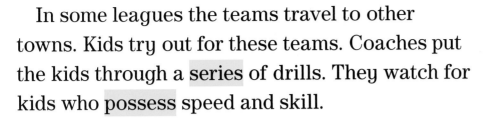

In some leagues the teams travel to other towns. Kids try out for these teams. Coaches put the kids through a series of drills. They watch for kids who possess speed and skill.

It takes more than skill to be a great athlete, though. It is also important to be a good sport. This means you treat others the way you would like to be treated. You show respect for your opponents. You do not want to challenge the referee's calls.

The spread of soccer has given numerous kids the chance to be part of a team. All players on a team have different skills. Even so, each team member can play as an equal.

Crossword Puzzle

Create a crossword puzzle with the vocabulary words. First, decide how you will have the words overlap. Then draw empty boxes for the letters. Create separate sets of clues for words that go "Across" and words that go "Down." Give your puzzle to a classmate to complete.

Concept Vocabulary

The concept term for this lesson is *peer pressure.* Peers are people who are the same age or in the same group. **Peer pressure** is when one or more members of the group try to influence another person in the group. The person feels pressure to act a certain way. Think of some ways peer pressure can have a positive influence. Then think of some ways it can have a negative influence. Talk about your ideas.

A **biography** is the story of a real person's life that is written by another person.

Comprehension Skill

Main Idea and Details

As you read, look for details that help show the main idea of the selection.

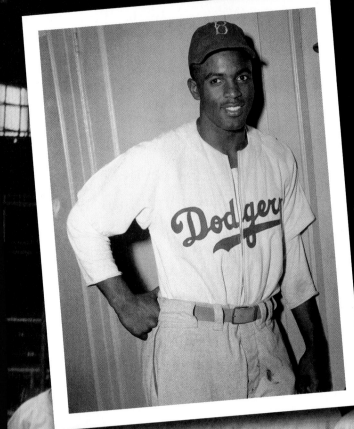

Focus Questions

Why must we sometimes show courage to keep a friend? Why is working together toward a common goal important to friendships?

Teammates

by Peter Golenbock
illustrated by Paul Bacon

Jackie Robinson

Pee Wee Reese

Jackie Robinson was more than just my teammate. He had a tremendous amount of talent, ability, and dedication. Jackie set a standard for future generations of ball players.

He was a winner.
Jackie Robinson was also a *man.*

—Pee Wee Reese

October 31, 1989

Once upon a time in America, when automobiles were black and looked like tanks and laundry was white and hung on clotheslines to dry, there were two wonderful baseball leagues that no longer exist. They were called the Negro Leagues.

The Negro Leagues had extraordinary players, and adoring fans came to see them wherever they played. They were heroes, but players in the Negro Leagues didn't make much money and their lives on the road were hard.

Laws against segregation didn't exist in the 1940s. In many places in this country, black people were not allowed to go to the same schools and churches as white people. They couldn't sit in the front of a bus or trolley car. They couldn't drink from the same drinking fountains that white people drank from.

Satchel Paige

Back then, many hotels didn't rent rooms to black people, so the Negro League players slept in their cars. Many towns had no restaurants that would serve them, so they often had to eat meals that they could buy and carry with them.

Life was very different for the players in the Major Leagues. They were the leagues for white players. Compared to the Negro League players, white players were very well paid. They stayed in good hotels and ate in fine restaurants. Their pictures were put on baseball cards and the best players became famous all over the world.

Branch Rickey

Many Americans knew that racial prejudice was wrong, but few dared to challenge openly the way things were. And many people were apathetic about racial problems. Some feared that it could be dangerous to object. Vigilante groups, like the Ku Klux Klan, reacted violently against those who tried to change the way blacks were treated.

The general manager of the Brooklyn Dodgers baseball team was a man by the name of Branch Rickey. He was not afraid of change. He wanted to treat the Dodger fans to the best players he could find, regardless of the color of their skin. He thought segregation was unfair and wanted to give everyone, regardless of race or creed, an opportunity to compete equally on ballfields across America.

Branch Rickey and Jackie Robinson

To do this, the Dodgers needed one special man.

Branch Rickey launched a search for him. He was looking for a star player in the Negro Leagues who would be able to compete successfully despite threats on his life or attempts to injure him. He would have to possess the self-control not to fight back when opposing players tried to intimidate or hurt him. If this man disgraced himself on the field, Rickey knew, his opponents would use it as an excuse to keep blacks out of Major League baseball for many more years.

Rickey thought Jackie Robinson might be just the man.

Jackie rode the train to Brooklyn to meet Mr. Rickey. When Mr. Rickey told him, "I want a man with the courage not to fight back," Jackie Robinson replied, "If you take this gamble, I will do my best to perform." They shook hands. Branch Rickey and Jackie Robinson were starting on what would be known in history as "the great experiment."

At spring training with the Dodgers, Jackie was mobbed by blacks, young and old, as if he were a savior. He was the first black player to try out for a Major League team. If he succeeded, they knew, others would follow.

Initially, life with the Dodgers was for Jackie a series of humiliations. The players on his team who came from the South, men who had been taught to avoid black people since childhood, moved to another table whenever he sat down next to them. Many opposing players were cruel to him, calling him nasty names from their dugouts. A few tried to hurt him with their spiked shoes. Pitchers aimed at his head. And he received threats on his life, both from individuals and from organizations like the Ku Klux Klan.

Jackie Robinson

Team photo of the 1947 Brooklyn Dodgers

Despite all the difficulties, Jackie Robinson didn't give up. He made the Brooklyn Dodgers team.

But making the Dodgers was only the beginning. Jackie had to face abuse and hostility throughout the season, from April through September. His worst pain was inside. Often he felt very alone. On the road he had to live by himself, because only the white players were allowed in the hotels in towns where the team played.

The whole time Pee Wee Reese, the Dodger shortstop, was growing up in Louisville, Kentucky, he had rarely even seen a black person, unless it was in the back of a bus. Most of his friends and relatives hated the idea of his playing on the same field as a black man. In addition, Pee Wee Reese had more to lose than the other players when Jackie joined the team.

118

Jackie had been a shortstop, and everyone thought that Jackie would take Pee Wee's job. Lesser men might have felt anger toward Jackie, but Pee Wee was different. He told himself, "If he's good enough to take my job, he deserves it."

When his Southern teammates circulated a petition to throw Jackie off the team and asked him to sign it, Pee Wee responded, "I don't care if this man is black, blue, or striped"—and refused to sign. "He can play and he can help us win," he told the others. "That's what counts."

Very early in the season, the Dodgers traveled west to Ohio to play the Cincinnati Reds. Cincinnati is near Pee Wee's hometown of Louisville.

The Reds played in a small ballpark where the fans sat close to the field. The players could almost feel the breath of the fans on the backs of their necks. Many who came that day screamed terrible, hateful things at Jackie when the Dodgers were on the field.

More than anything else, Pee Wee Reese believed in doing what was right. When he heard the fans yelling at Jackie, Pee Wee decided to take a stand.

With his head high, Pee Wee walked directly from his shortstop position to where Jackie was playing first base. The taunts and shouting of the fans were ringing in Pee Wee's ears. It saddened him, because he knew it could have been his friends and neighbors. Pee Wee's legs felt heavy, but he knew what he had to do.

As he walked toward Jackie wearing the gray Dodger uniform, he looked into his teammate's bold, pained eyes. The first baseman had done nothing to provoke the hostility except that he sought to be treated as an equal. Jackie was grim with anger. Pee Wee smiled broadly as he reached Jackie. Jackie smiled back.

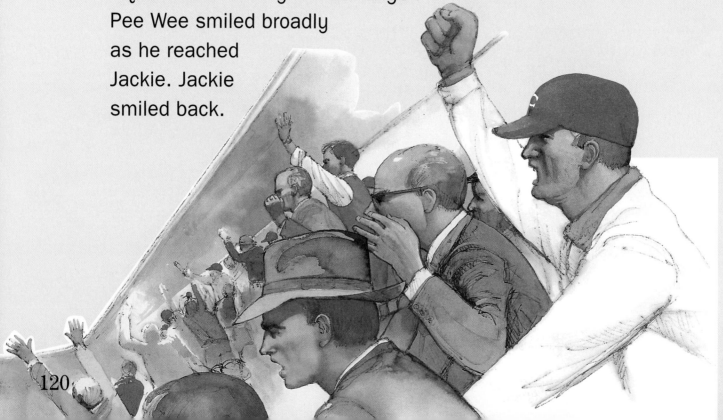

Stopping beside Jackie, Pee Wee put his arm around Jackie's shoulders. An audible gasp rose up from the crowd when they saw what Pee Wee had done. Then there was silence.

Outlined on a sea of green grass stood these two great athletes, one black, one white, both wearing the same team uniform.

"I am standing by him," Pee Wee Reese said to the world. "This man is my teammate."

Meet the Author

Peter Golenbock

Peter Golenbock is a famous sports writer whose books have been best sellers. He started writing, in part, because of his love for baseball. Golenbock has also been a sports-radio, talk-show host and a broadcaster for baseball. He and his wife and son live in St. Petersburg, Florida.

Meet the Illustrator

Paul Bacon

Paul Bacon has many interests, including writing, drawing cartoons, and photography. Bacon is known as being both funny and well-traveled. He has lived in eighteen cities, including two in Japan. He has also traveled to more than thirty countries, from Australia to Uzbekistan.

Friendship

Theme Connections

Within the Selection

1. How did Pee Wee Reese show Jackie Robinson his friendship?

2. Why was Pee Wee's friendship so important to Jackie?

Across Selections

3. How is friendship in this story like friendship in "The Legend of Damon and Pythias"?

4. What other selections tell about courage and loyalty in a friendship?

Beyond the Selection

5. Why is loyalty important in friendships?

6. Have you ever had a friend stand up for you in a difficult time?

Write about It!

Describe a time when you stood up for a friend.

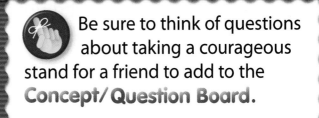

Be sure to think of questions about taking a courageous stand for a friend to add to the **Concept/Question Board.**

Social Studies Inquiry

Guiding the Way to Freedom

Genre

A **biography** is the story of a real person's life that is written by another person.

Feature

A **time line** shows the order in which important events happened.

Harriet Tubman was born as a slave. However, even as a young girl, she was determined to be free. She wanted a better life.

Tubman worked hard. She was a maid and a nanny. She split wood and loaded it onto wagons.

Like many slaves, Tubman was not treated well. Her clothes were thin and ragged. She had little food to eat. Her owners were mean and unfair.

As a teen, Tubman heard rumors. She learned that some slaves had run away. They escaped to the North, where they could be free.

Many people were opposed to slavery. These people set up a system to help slaves escape, called the Underground Railroad.

This railroad did not have trains or tracks. It was a series of houses where slaves could hide, eat, and rest.

Harriet Tubman used the Underground Railroad. She escaped when she was about 30 years old. She then helped others escape to freedom.

Tubman took great risks. Runaway slaves would be punished if they were caught. This did not stop Tubman. She made 19 trips back to the South and helped more than 300 slaves escape.

Think Link

Time Line of Harriet Tubman's Life

1857: rescues parents from slavery

1849: escapes on Underground Railroad

1870: marries Nelson Davis

1913: dies in New York

1820: born Harriet Ross in Maryland

1850: makes first of 19 trips as guide for runaway slaves

1906: builds a home for the sick and needy

1844: marries John Tubman

1. How does the time line add to your understanding of the text?

2. What was the purpose of the Underground Railroad?

3. Think of two adjectives that describe Harriet Tubman. Explain why you chose those words.

Try It!

As you work on your investigation, think about how you can use a time line to tell more about your topic.

New Neighbors

by Bobbi Katz

illustrated by Marion Eldridge

A family's moving into the house
   across the street, I see.
A Mom, a Dad, and three
   weird kids—
One might be the same age as me.
His sister is too little.
His brother is too tall.
That middle kid might be in
   my class.
I'm sure I won't like him at all.
Oh no, he's coming up our stairs.
He's ringing our front bell.
I know that I won't like him.
Already I can tell.

Well yes. I'm glad to meet you, too.
   Do I trade baseball cards? I do.
You'll be in Mrs. Warren's class.
   Yes, she gives tests. Keep cool.
   You'll pass.
I'll show you around the
   neighborhood.
   Tomorrow morning? That
   sounds good.
A family moved into the house
   across the street today.
José, their kid, will be my friend.
   I knew it right away.

Since Hanna Moved Away

by Judith Viorst

illustrated by Marion Eldridge

The tires on my bike are flat.
The sky is grouchy gray.
At least it sure feels like that
Since Hanna moved away.

Chocolate ice cream tastes like
  prunes.
December's come to stay.
They've taken back the Mays
  and Junes
Since Hanna moved away.

Flowers smell like halibut.
Velvet feels like hay.
Every handsome dog's a mutt
Since Hanna moved away.

Nothing's fun to laugh about.
Nothing's fun to play.
They call me, but I won't come out
Since Hanna moved away.

127

Test Prep

Test-Taking Strategy: Following Directions

When you take a test, read the directions carefully so you know what you are supposed to do. You will have to answer different kinds of questions on a test. Following directions carefully will help you choose the right answers.

Following Directions

Here are some sample directions. Read them carefully. Think about what the directions are telling you.

> **Read the directions for this question carefully. Think about the answer.**
>
> Which two words have the SAME meaning?
> Ⓐ angry, happy
> Ⓑ late, busy
> Ⓒ run, swim
> Ⓓ small, tiny

The last answer is correct because *small* and *tiny* mean about the same thing. One answer is two words that are opposites, and another is two words that are sports. The best way to answer this question correctly is to read it carefully.

Whenever you take a test, be sure to read the directions carefully. The directions will help you answer the questions correctly.

Test-Taking Practice

Read the story "Friends for Life." Then answer numbers 1 through 4.

"Oh Lu . . . cee. Oh Lu . . . cee. Can you come out to play?" This is what Dora called out every day after school.

Lucy and Dora were friends. Lucy had dark hair and looked very different from her friend. Dora had blonde hair and lived two houses away from Lucy.

Dora was shy but friendly. Lucy was loud and funny. Dora had four sisters. They each had different colored hair and eyes. Lucy liked them because they all looked very different from each other.

All of Lucy's brothers and sisters were older. They were not often home to play with her. This made Lucy feel like an only child. She did not feel that way around Dora and her sisters. Dora's family treated Lucy as if she were part of their family. The family took Lucy to the library, to the beach, and other places.

The best thing that Dora's family did was help Lucy learn English. Lucy's family spoke another language at home. Lucy could speak both languages. Even so, she wanted to speak English better.

Dora and her sisters would help Lucy say different words. They never made fun of her. One thing they did was play school. Lucy also learned not to be afraid to ask for help. Dora and her sisters helped Lucy feel good about herself.

One day, a sad thing happened. Dora and her family moved. Dora would be going to a different school. Lucy cried a lot when she heard the news.

After a few days, Lucy did not feel so gloomy any more. She missed Dora and her sisters, but she made more friends. Her English was very good now. She was even able to help some other girls and boys in school.

Lucy and Dora stayed friends for many, many years. They grew up and got married. Each of them had families. Their children became friends. Whenever Dora and her family came to visit, they did something funny. They would all say, "Oh Lu . . . cee. Can you come out to play?"

Use what you learned from the story "Friends for Life" to answer Numbers 1 through 4. Write your answers on a piece of paper.

Test Tips

- Read the directions carefully.

- Look at each answer.

- Mark your answer carefully.

1. Which would be another good title for this story?

   Ⓐ "Playing Outside"

   Ⓑ "Part of the Family"

   Ⓒ "Moving"

   Ⓓ "A Different School"

2. What made Lucy feel like part of Dora's family?

   Ⓐ Dora's sisters all looked different.

   Ⓑ Dora's family helped her learn new words.

   Ⓒ Dora's family took her with them to visit places.

   Ⓓ Dora's sisters and Lucy played school.

3. Dora and her children say, "Oh Lu . . . cee. Can you come out to play?" because

   Ⓐ Dora is too shy to talk to Lucy by herself.

   Ⓑ Lucy only comes out to play if they ask her to.

   Ⓒ they do not know how to say Lucy's name.

   Ⓓ that is how Dora has always called to Lucy.

4. Why did the author begin the story with "Oh Lu . . . cee"?

   Ⓐ To show how Dora called Lucy

   Ⓑ To help the reader remember her name

   Ⓒ To say something funny

   Ⓓ To get ready for the ending of the story

Animals and Their Habitats

Do you ever stop to wonder about where animals live? Pets live in our homes, but what about animals in nature? They have their own special habitats. It is important to learn about and respect the homes of the many different animals in our world.

Theme Connection

Look at the photograph. What habitat is portrayed here? What animals do you see? What other animals live in this habitat? How do they share the habitat?

BIG
Idea

Where do different
animals live?

133

Genre

Expository Text is nonfiction that is written to inform, to explain, or to persuade.

Comprehension Strategy

⭐ **Clarifying** As you read, ask yourself questions about things or ideas in the selection that you do not understand.

One Small Place in a Tree

Focus Questions

How are certain changes in a habitat good for some animals but not for others? How might a tree be a home to many kinds of animals?

by Barbara Brenner
Illustrated by Tom Leonard

Read the article to find the meanings of these words, which are also in "One Small Place in a Tree":

✦ hollow
✦ dwellers
✦ maze
✦ stored
✦ except
✦ swarming
✦ bacteria

Vocabulary Strategy

Context Clues are hints in the text. They help you find the meanings of words. Use context clues to find the meaning of *hollow*.

Vocabulary
Warm-Up

Most kinds of bees live alone, but not honeybees. These social insects live and work in a hive. In the wild, bees often build hives in a hollow tree trunk or log. They find these empty spaces on their own. Honeybees do not bore into the wood to make a hive.

Have you heard the phrase "busy as a bee"? Bees actually do work hard. Each of the hive-dwellers has at least one job. As you might suppose, the most active bees are called "workers." Workers build, clean, and guard the hive. They also gather food and water.

Workers make wax in their bodies. They use the wax to build a complex maze of cells. Honey and pollen are stored in some of these cells. Eggs are laid in others.

No bee except the queen can lay eggs; each hive has only one queen bee. Worker bees feed the queen as well as small, growing bees in the hive. Workers also feed the drones. Drones are male bees.

You may not welcome the sight of swarming bees, but honeybees help humans in many ways. They pollinate flowers and trees. This allows seeds and fruit to be produced. Even the honey provided by the bees is more than a sweet food. It has also been used as a folk remedy because of its ability to kill bacteria.

GAME

Definition Game

With a small group of classmates, play a game to review the meaning of each vocabulary word. The game starts with one player giving a definition. The player might say, "What word means 'persons or animals living in a place'?" The classmate who correctly names the vocabulary word (*dwellers*) gets to choose the next definition to give to the group. Play until all of the vocabulary words have been used.

Concept Vocabulary

The concept word for this lesson is *shelter.* **Shelter** is something that covers or protects from weather or danger. How do animals in the wild find shelter? What are some ways that humans help provide shelter for wild animals? Do you think this is a good idea?

Genre

Expository Text is nonfiction that is written to inform, to explain, or to persuade.

Comprehension Strategy

Clarifying
As you read, ask yourself questions about things or ideas in the selection that you do not understand.

Focus Questions

How are certain changes in a habitat good for some animals but not for others? How might a tree be a home to many kinds of animals?

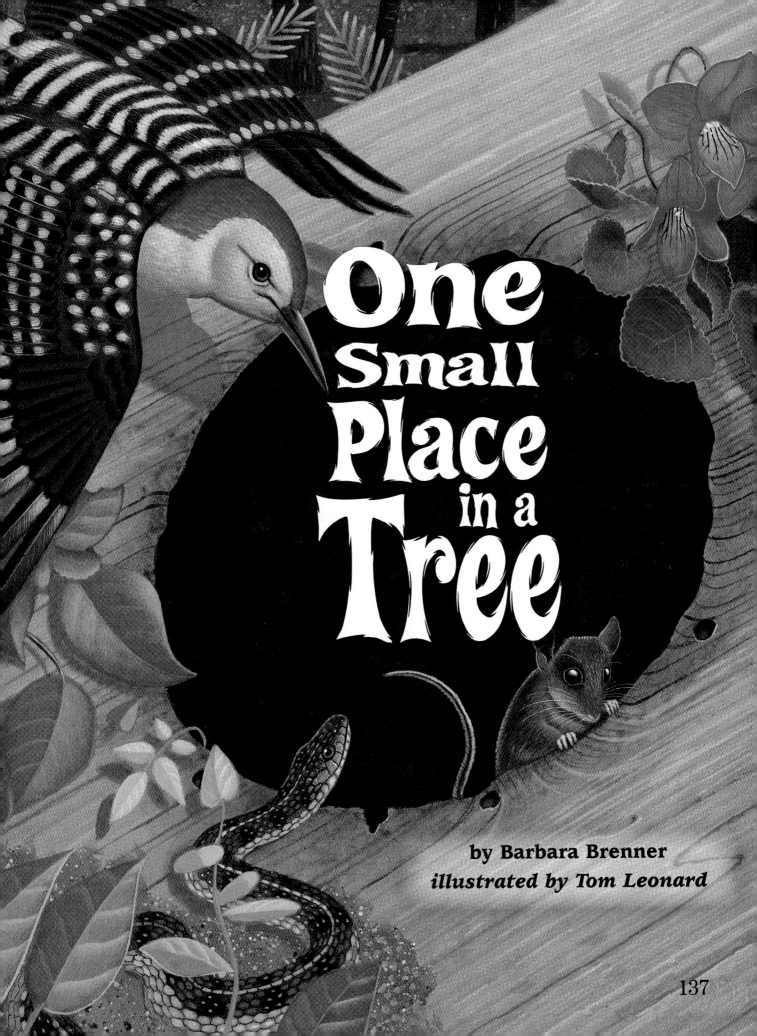

One Small Place in a Tree

by Barbara Brenner

illustrated by Tom Leonard

A tree hole. One small place in a tree. How does it get there? Who lives inside?

Suppose that you could watch a hole from its beginning. You might see something like this:

Here's one oak tree in a forest. It looks like the others, except—a black bear uses this one as a scratching post. Every time she goes by, the bear sharpens her claws on the trunk.

You're walking in the woods. You see the tree and notice the scratch marks on the bark. Maybe you even catch a glimpse of the bear!

After a while the scratching chips some pieces of bark off the tree. A cut forms in the bark. A hole in the tree is beginning.

Next time you're walking there, you see that tiny bugs have found the cut. They're timber beetles, and they're about to set up housekeeping.

The timber beetles get under the bark and bore into the tree. They make a maze of tunnels. They create spaces called cradles for their eggs. And they "plant" fungi for the colony to feed on. Imagine that you can look inside. You see something like this.

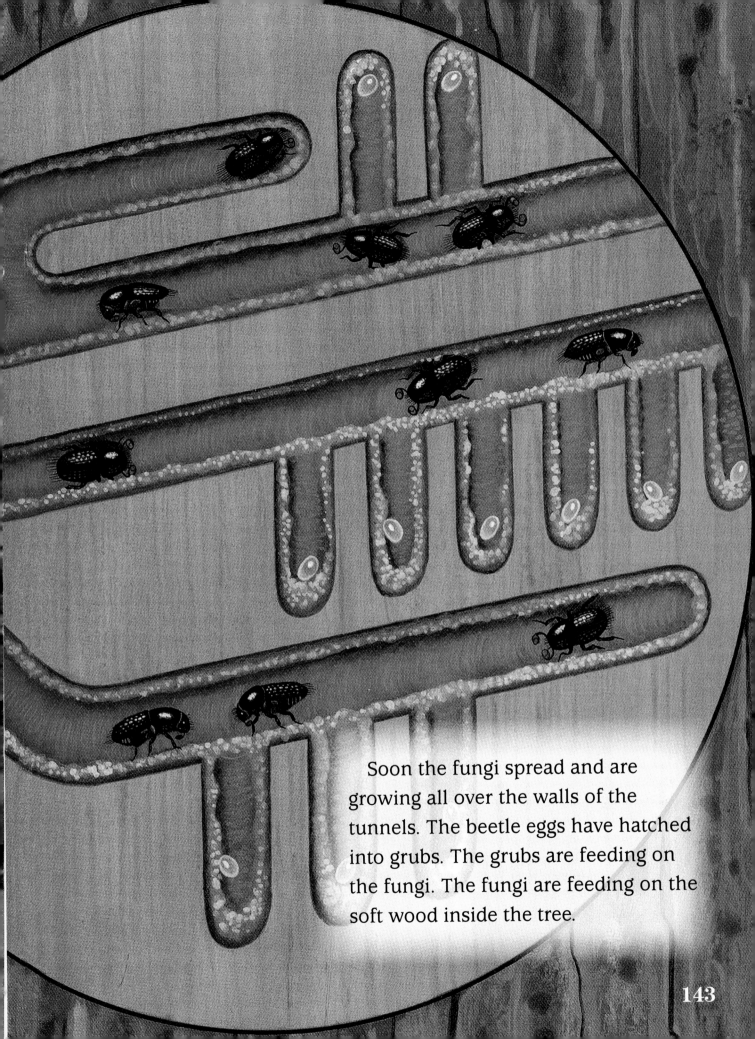

Soon the fungi spread and are growing all over the walls of the tunnels. The beetle eggs have hatched into grubs. The grubs are feeding on the fungi. The fungi are feeding on the soft wood inside the tree.

143

Now disease strikes. Bacteria come in through the hole in the tree. You won't see the bacteria—they're too small. But you can see the damage they've done. The tree has heart rot. It's dying inside and out.

Bark begins to loosen and fall off. The hole is now so large that you can actually see inside. It has become a hollow place that looks as if it could be home for something.

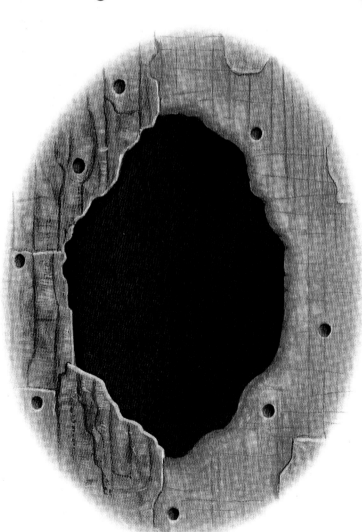

The first animal to use it is a flying squirrel. You find the squirrel "holed up" in there one winter day. You notice that it has stored some nuts under the loose bark around the hole.

147

When you come by in the spring, the flying squirrel is gone. The hole is empty, but not for long. A pair of bluebirds moves in. The hole is just right for bluebirds— high enough off the ground for safety.

The bluebirds line the hole with weeds and grass. Soon there are six bluish eggs in the nest hole.

Next time you look inside, there are six bluebird chicks. The chicks stay safe in the nest until they're old enough to fly.

149

By this time the oak tree is no longer sending out leaves. Almost all of its bark is gone. But the hole-dwellers don't seem to care.

For the next three springs, the hole in the tree is a nest for the same pair of bluebirds.

For the next three winters, it's home to a family of white-footed mice.

In all those three years, the tree hasn't grown at all. This oak tree is dead. But—the hole is full of life.

A hairy woodpecker sometimes comes to roost there.

A gray squirrel often uses the hole as a hiding place.

When the hole has water in it, you can sometimes see a tree frog there.

One day lightning, or a high wind, or heavy rain, or snow will bring this dead tree down. Many years later all that may be left will be a log with a hole in it.

But the hole will still be a place for living things. A small garter snake may cool off in there.

A redback salamander may lay its eggs there.

Or maybe a hammock spider will make a web across the hole to catch swarming insects.

Living trees are important. But so are dead and dying trees. A dead tree often has a hole—one small place that is usually home for something.

Meet the Author

Barbara Brenner

Barbara Brenner likes poetry, art, science, animals, and nature. She writes stories that come from both her imagination and from real life. Over the years, Brenner has written over 70 children's books and has won many awards. She and her husband live in Pennsylvania.

Meet the Illustrator

Tom Leonard

Tom Leonard studied art at the Philadelphia College of Art. He has worked as an illustrator for newspapers and magazines, and is now illustrating children's books. He likes to draw pictures of nature using bright colors. Leonard taught art at the Philadelphia University of the Arts and often visits schools to talk about his work.

Animals and Their Habitats

Theme Connections

Within the Selection

1. What different forms of life have lived in the tree?

2. What might happen if lightning struck the tree?

Beyond the Selection

3. What does "One Small Place in a Tree" tell you about animals and their habitats?

4. What are some other animal habitats?

Write about It!

Describe an animal habitat you have seen near your home or school.

Remember to look for pictures of animal habitats to add to the **Concept/ Question Board.**

Science Inquiry

Please Feed the Birds

Birds use energy at a fast rate. Therefore, they need high-energy foods to replace what they burn. Insects are a main food source for many kinds of birds. However, in fall and winter, once-swarming insects can become scarce. So some bird lovers help their feathered friends stay fed.

Suet, or raw beef fat, is a great high-energy food for birds. Stores sell packaged suet cakes, but you can make your own. Homemade cakes can be made with beef fat purchased from a grocery store. If you want to try this recipe, ask an adult for help. **Never turn on a stove by yourself!**

Hard Suet Cakes

$\frac{1}{2}$ pound fresh ground suet

$\frac{1}{3}$ cup sunflower seed

$\frac{2}{3}$ cup wild birdseed mix

$\frac{1}{8}$ cup chopped peanuts

$\frac{1}{4}$ cup raisins

1. Melt the suet in a pan over low heat. Allow it to cool, and then reheat it.

2. Mix the rest of the ingredients in a large bowl.

3. Let the suet cool until it starts to get thick; then stir it into the mixture in the bowl. Mix well.

4. Pour into a pie pan or square mold to cool.

When the suet cakes are cool and hard, put them in a feeder. The most common type of suet feeder is a small wire cage. Attach the cage to a tree trunk, or hang it from a branch. Suet cakes can be stored in a freezer for up to three months.

Think Link

1. Why can winter be a difficult time for some birds?

2. Why is the last line of text in paragraph 2 emphasized?

3. How is the list of ingredients helpful?

Try It!

As you work on your investigation, think about how you can use bold type to emphasize an important sentence in your final presentation.

Read the story to find the meanings of these words, which are also in "Make Way for Ducklings":

◆ beckoned
◆ responsibility
◆ enormous
◆ hatch
◆ strange
◆ bringing up

Vocabulary Strategy

Apposition is when a word or group of words define another word in the same sentence. Use apposition to find the meaning of *enormous*.

Vocabulary

Warm-Up

Drew was riding his bike when Mrs. Fultz beckoned from her front porch. She and Mr. Fultz were taking a short trip and needed someone to feed the chickens. Drew agreed to take on the responsibility.

The next day Drew returned to Fultz Farm. He pushed with all his might to slide open the enormous, or very big, wooden door to the barn. Inside, Drew found the barrel of feed and scooped a bucketful.

As Drew scattered the feed, the chickens went to work! They strutted from place to place and pecked greedily. But one hen stayed put on her cozy nest.

Drew tried to approach the nesting hen. When he got close, the hen ruffled her feathers. That was when Drew saw the eggs.

It looked as if some of the eggs were cracked. The chicks would soon hatch! Drew was sure he did not want to miss this. He turned over the bucket to make a chair that suited him just fine.

Over the next hour, Drew watched as six chicks emerged from their shells. He cheered each one as it entered its strange, new world. He looked on as their wet, sticky feathers dried and fluffed up.

Finally, Drew headed for home. He seemed to be extra aware of life around him. He heard the bullfrogs' deep voices down by the pond. He saw squirrels running up the side of an oak tree.

Drew realized how glad he was that his parents had moved next to Fultz Farm. They always said the country was a good place for bringing up kids. Now, Drew could not agree more.

GAME

Making Sentences

Work with a partner to create sentences using the vocabulary words. Choose two words from the list, and challenge your partner to make up a sentence using the two words. Then switch roles. Continue until all of the vocabulary words have been used.

Concept Vocabulary

The concept word for this lesson is *environment.* **Environment** is the surroundings that affect living things. An environment includes objects, activities, weather, and other conditions. Compare your environment at home with your environment at school. How are they alike? How are they different?

Genre

A **fantasy** is a fictional story that could not happen in real life. Fantasy stories may have characters that do things or tell of things that could not happen in real life.

Comprehension Skill

 Reality and Fantasy

As you read, identify examples of reality and fantasy in the story.

Make Way

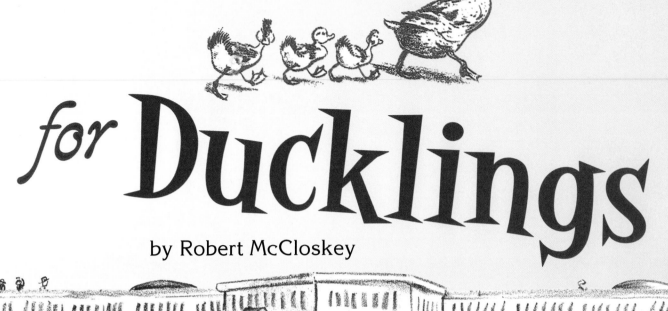

for Ducklings

by Robert McCloskey

Focus Questions

How do various types of city wildlife adapt to their environments? What roles do people play in protecting the natural environment?

Mr. and Mrs. Mallard were looking for a place to live. But every time Mr. Mallard saw what looked like a nice place, Mrs. Mallard said it was no good. There were sure to be foxes in the woods or turtles in the water, and she was not going to raise a family where there might be foxes or turtles. So they flew on and on.

When they got to Boston, they felt too tired to fly any further. There was a nice pond in the Public Garden, with a little island on it. "The very place to spend the night," quacked Mr. Mallard. So down they flapped.

Next morning they fished for their breakfast in the mud at the bottom of the pond. But they didn't find much.

Just as they were getting ready to start on their way, a strange enormous bird came by. It was pushing a boat full of people, and there was a man sitting on its back. "Good morning," quacked Mr. Mallard, being polite. The big bird was too proud to answer. But the people on the boat threw peanuts into the water, so the Mallards followed them all round the pond and got another breakfast, better than the first.

"I like this place," said Mrs. Mallard as they climbed out on the bank and waddled along. "Why don't we build a nest and raise our ducklings right in this pond? There are no foxes and no turtles, and the people feed us peanuts. What could be better?"

"Good," said Mr. Mallard, delighted that at last Mrs. Mallard had found a place that suited her. But—

"Look out!" squawked Mrs. Mallard, all of a dither. "You'll get run over!" And when she got her breath she added: "*This* is no place for babies, with all those horrid things rushing about. We'll have to look somewhere else."

So they flew over Beacon Hill and round the State House, but there was no place there.

They looked in Louisburg Square, but there was no water to swim in.

Then they flew over the Charles River. "This is better," quacked Mr. Mallard. "That island looks like a nice quiet place, and it's only a little way from the Public Garden." "Yes," said Mrs. Mallard, remembering the peanuts. "That looks like just the right place to hatch ducklings."

So they chose a cozy spot among the bushes near the water and settled down to build their nest. And only just in time, for now they were beginning to molt. All their old wing feathers started to drop out, and they would not be able to fly again until the new ones grew in.

But of course they could swim, and one day they swam over to the park on the river bank, and there they met a policeman called Michael. Michael fed them peanuts, and after that the Mallards called on Michael every day.

After Mrs. Mallard had laid eight eggs in the nest she couldn't go to visit Michael any more, because she had to sit on the eggs to keep them warm. She moved off the nest only to get a drink of water, or to have her lunch, or to count the eggs and make sure they were all there.

One day the ducklings hatched out. First came Jack, then Kack, and then Lack, then Mack and Nack and Ouack and Pack and Quack. Mr. and Mrs. Mallard were bursting with pride. It was a great

165

responsibility taking care of so many ducklings, and it kept them very busy.

One day Mr. Mallard decided he'd like to take a trip to see what the rest of the river was like, further on. So off he set. "I'll meet you in a week, in the Public Garden," he quacked over his shoulder. "Take good care of the ducklings."

"Don't you worry," said Mrs. Mallard. "I know all about bringing up children." And she did.

She taught them how to swim and dive.

She taught them to walk in a line, to come when they were called, and to keep a safe distance from bikes and scooters and other things with wheels.

When at last she felt perfectly satisfied with them, she said one morning: "Come along, children. Follow me." Before you could wink an eyelash Jack, Kack, Lack, Mack, Nack, Ouack, Pack, and Quack fell into line, just as they had been taught. Mrs. Mallard led the way into the water and they swam behind her to the opposite bank.

There they waded ashore and waddled along till they came to the highway.

Mrs. Mallard stepped out to cross the road. "Honk, honk!" went the horns on the speeding cars. "Qua-a-ack!" went Mrs. Mallard as she tumbled back again. "Quack! Quack! Quack! Quack!" went Jack, Kack, Lack, Mack, Nack, Ouack, Pack, and Quack, just as loud as their little quackers could quack. The cars kept speeding by and honking, and Mrs. Mallard and the ducklings kept right on quack-quack-quacking.

They made such a noise that Michael came running, waving his arms and blowing his whistle.

He planted himself in the center of the road, raised one hand to stop the traffic, and then beckoned with the other, the way policemen do, for Mrs. Mallard to cross over.

As soon as Mrs. Mallard and the ducklings were safe on the other side and on their way down Mount Vernon Street, Michael rushed back to his police booth.

He called Clancy at headquarters and said: "There's a family of ducks walkin' down the street!" Clancy said: "Family of *what?*" "*Ducks!*" yelled Michael. "Send a police car, quick!"

Meanwhile Mrs. Mallard had reached the Corner Book Shop and turned into Charles Street, with Jack, Kack, Lack, Mack, Nack, Ouack, Pack, and Quack all marching in line behind her.

Everyone stared. An old lady from Beacon Hill said: "Isn't it

amazing!" and the man who swept the streets said: "Well, now, ain't that nice!" and when Mrs. Mallard heard them she was so proud she tipped her nose in the air and walked along with an extra swing in her waddle.

When they came to the corner of Beacon Street there was the police car with four policemen that Clancy had sent from headquarters. The policemen held back the traffic so Mrs. Mallard and the ducklings could march across the street, right on into the Public Garden.

Inside the gate they all turned round to say thank you to the policemen. The policemen smiled and waved good-by.

When they reached the pond and swam across to the little island, there was Mr. Mallard waiting for them, just as he had promised.

The ducklings liked the new island so much that they decided to live there. All day long they follow the swan boats and eat peanuts.

And when night falls they swim to their little island and go to sleep.

Robert McCloskey

Robert McCloskey changed his mind many times before he settled on a career. He learned to play several instruments in the hopes of being a musician. He later thought he would be an inventor because he liked to work with mechanical things. Then he began drawing and became very good at it. To prepare for writing *Make Way for Ducklings*, McCloskey bought four mallard ducks, which he kept in his apartment to observe and sketch. It took him two years to plan what he wanted to write about, and another two years to write and draw the story. His hard work and patience paid off. He won a Caldecott Medal, an important award for Children's books, for *Make Way for Ducklings*.

Animals and Their Habitats
Theme Connections

Within the Selection

1. What was important to Mr. and Mrs. Mallard as they looked for a home in the city?

2. How did the people in the story help protect Mr. and Mrs. Mallard and their family?

Across Selections

3. How is this selection like "One Small Place in a Tree"?

4. How is it different?

Beyond the Selection

5. What does "Make Way for Ducklings" tell you about animals and their habitats?

6. What can you do to help protect animals that live in your neighborhood?

Write about It!

Describe a time you helped an animal.

Remember to look for articles about people helping animals in their habitats to add to the **Concept/Question Board.**

Science Inquiry

Frozen Frogs

Genre

Expository Text tells people something. It contains facts about real people or events.

Feature

A **diagram** adds to information provided in the text. Some diagrams show a process.

Wood frogs live all over North America. In much of this region, winter brings freezing temperatures. Some animals migrate to escape the cold. Others tunnel in the ground, below the frost line. The wood frog does something strange: it freezes!

When cold weather sets in, the wood frog finds a good place to spend the winter, usually under a pile of damp leaves. Then the freezing process starts.

When the frog's body gets close to the freezing mark, its heart rate slows. Then the frog's blood and body tissues start to freeze. At last, ice forms around and inside the heart. Frozen solid, the heart stops beating.

In the spring, as temperatures rise, the frog starts to thaw. First, the heart beats again. Ice on the skin melts, then evaporates. Blood becomes liquid and flows again. The leg muscles soften. Within one day, the frog's body is back to normal.

The thawed frog looks for a small, shallow pond formed by melted snow and ice. A temporary pond such as this is a good place for the wood frog to lay its eggs. These ponds do not have fish that would eat the eggs before they can hatch.

Wood frogs are active through the summer and fall. They eat and build up body fat. Then, when winter comes again, they take their chilly time-out.

Think Link   Seasonal Changes of the Wood Frog

Fall
The wood frog is active at any time of day. Its body stores fat.

Summer
The wood frog rests in the day and hunts for food at night, when it is cooler.

Winter
The wood frog crawls under leaf litter on the ground. Its body freezes solid.

Spring
The wood frog thaws. Females lay eggs in ponds made by melting snow and ice.

1. What are some of the ways animals survive cold winter weather?

2. In what kind of environment does the wood frog live?

3. Why are arrows used in the diagram?

Try It!

As you work on your investigation, think about how you can use a diagram to explain a process.

Read the story to find the meanings of these words, which are also in "Wolf Island":

✦ mild
✦ layer
✦ mainland
✦ population
✦ balance
✦ aboard
✦ male
✦ female

Vocabulary Strategy

Word Structure is when parts of a word help you understand the word's meaning. Use word structure to find the meaning of *mainland*.

Vocabulary
Warm-Up

Clare checked her suitcase one more time. She had all she needed for her trip to the island. She could not wait to spend the weekend with her cousin Holly on Loon Island!

Dad rode the ferry over with Clare. It was a mild day, which made for a smooth crossing. The bottom layer of the ferry had an enclosed space. But Clare and Dad went to the top deck for some fresh air.

Holly met Clare and Dad at the dock. She was just as excited as Clare. And she was happy to have some help in her job. Holly was a "loon watcher."

Dad said his hellos and good-byes, then rode the ferry back to the mainland. Holly and Clare set to work. As loon watchers, they helped

to monitor the birds' population. They kept a log of the number of loons they saw. They kept an eye out for loon nests.

Clare enjoyed the task. For her, being a loon watcher was a balance of work and fun. She loved to watch a parent loon act as a raft for its chicks. The babies would often climb aboard Mom or Dad for a lift! The chicks depended on their parents not just for a ride, but for protection.

Clare knew the loons' various calls. There was the yodel, the hoot, and the tremolo. Then there was the wail—the lonely sound of a male loon, or a female, looking for its mate or its chicks.

Sunday came too soon for Clare. She was not ready to return home. As the ferry drifted away from Loon Island, Clare heard a mournful wail. She understood the feeling.

GAME

Crossword Puzzle

Create a crossword puzzle with the vocabulary words. First, decide how you will have the words overlap. Then draw empty boxes for the letters. Create separate sets of clues for words that go "Across" and words that go "Down." Give your puzzle to a classmate to complete.

Concept Vocabulary

The concept word for this lesson is *wildlife.* **Wildlife** is living things, especially animals, in their natural environments. How do different species of wildlife depend on each other for survival?

Making Inferences

As you read, make inferences by connecting information from the story to what you already know.

Wolf

Focus Questions

What are ways that different animals help make a habitat successful? How might your habitat be affected if an important part was removed?

Island

by Celia Godkin

Once there was an island. It was an island with trees and meadows, and many kinds of animals. There were mice, rabbits and deer, squirrels, foxes and several kinds of birds.

All the animals on the island depended on the plants and the other animals for their food and well-being. Some animals ate grass or other plants; some ate insects; some ate other animals. The island animals were healthy. There was plenty of food for all.

A family of wolves lived on the island, too, a male wolf, a female, and their five cubs.

One day the wolf cubs were playing on the beach while their mother and father slept. The cubs found a strange object at the edge of the water.

It was a log raft, nailed together with boards. The cubs had never seen anything like this before. They were very curious. They climbed onto it and sniffed about. Everything smelled different.

While the cubs were poking around, the raft began to drift slowly out into the lake. At first the cubs didn't notice anything wrong. Then, suddenly, there was nothing but water all around the raft.

The cubs were scared. They howled. The mother and father wolf heard the howling and came running down to the water's edge.

They couldn't turn the raft back, and the cubs were too scared to swim, so the adult wolves swam out to the raft and climbed aboard. The raft drifted slowly and steadily over to the mainland. Finally it came to rest on the shore and the wolf family scrambled onto dry land.

There were no longer wolves on the island.

Time passed. Spring grew into summer on the island, and summer into fall. The leaves turned red. Geese flew south, and squirrels stored up nuts for the winter.

Winter was mild that year, with little snow. The green plants were buried under a thin white layer. Deer dug through the snow to find food. They had enough to eat.

Next spring, many fawns were born.

There were now many deer on the island. They were eating large amounts of grass and leaves. The wolf family had kept the deer population down, because wolves eat deer for food. Without wolves to hunt the deer, there were now too many deer on the island for the amount of food available.

Spring grew into summer and summer into fall. More and more deer ate more and more grass and more and more leaves.

Rabbits had less to eat, because the deer were eating their food. There were not many baby bunnies born that year.

Foxes had less to eat, because there were fewer rabbits for them to hunt.

Mice had less to eat, because the deer had eaten the grass and grass seed. There were not many baby mice born that year.

Owls had less to eat, because there were fewer mice for them to hunt. Many animals on the island were hungry.

The first snow fell. Squirrels curled
up in their holes, wrapped their tails
around them for warmth, and went to
sleep. The squirrels were lucky. They
had collected a store of nuts for winter.

Other animals did not have winter
stores. They had to find food in the
snow. Winter is a hard time for animals,
but this winter was harder than most.
The snow was deep and the weather
cold. Most of the plants had already
been eaten during the summer and fall.
Those few that remained were hard to
find, buried deep under the snow.

Rabbits were hungry. Foxes were hungry. Mice were hungry. Owls were hungry. Even the deer were hungry. The whole island was hungry.

The owls flew over to the mainland, looking for mice. They flew over the wolf family walking along the mainland shore. The wolves were thin and hungry, too. They had not found a home, because there were other wolf families on the mainland. The other wolves did not want to share with them.

Snow fell for many weeks. The drifts became deeper and deeper. It was harder and harder for animals to find food. Animals grew weaker, and some began to die. The deer were so hungry they gnawed bark from the trees. Trees began to die.

Snow covered the island. The weather grew colder and colder. Ice began to form in the water around the island, and along the mainland coast. It grew thicker and thicker, spreading farther and farther out into the open water. One day there was ice all the way from the mainland to the island.

The wolf family crossed the ice
and returned to their old home.

The wolves were hungry when they reached the island, and there were many weak and sick deer for them to eat. The wolves left the healthy deer alone.

Finally, spring came. The snow melted, and grass and leaves began to grow. The wolves remained in their island home, hunting deer. No longer would there be too many deer on the island. Grass and trees would grow again. Rabbits would find enough food. The mice would find enough food. There would be food for the foxes and owls. And there would be food for the deer. The island would have food enough for all.

Life on the island was
back in balance.

189

Meet the Author and Illustrator

Celia Godkin

Celia Godkin grew up in Brazil
and England and now lives in an
old farmhouse in Eastern Canada.
Science has always fascinated her.
While working at a zoo, Godkin got
the chance to help make a book about
Canada's endangered wildlife. She has
since worked on many projects that
combine her talents as a writer and
illustrator with her love of science.

Animals and Their Habitats
Theme Connections

Within the Selection

1. How did the habitat change on the island?

2. What finally brought the habitat back into balance?

Across Selections

3. How is the animal habitat in "Wolf Island" like the animal habitat in "One Small Place in a Tree"?

4. How is it different?

Beyond the Selection

5. How might you cause change in an animal habitat?

6. How could you tell that you are causing change?

Write about It!

Describe how the animals on the island lived after the wolves left.

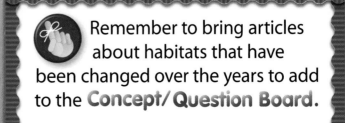

Remember to bring articles about habitats that have been changed over the years to add to the **Concept/Question Board.**

Science Inquiry

Ancient Wolves

Genre

Research Notes are a way to organize information about a topic you are studying.

Feature

Headings tell what kind of information is to follow.

When you write a research report, you need to gather information. You will take notes on what you read. Note cards, like the ones on these pages, can help you get organized. Here are notes one student took on the research topic "dire wolves."

What is a dire wolf?

The dire wolf is the largest known member of the wolf family. It lived during the Ice Age. The dire wolf would hunt for food or eat prey killed by other animals. This wolf is now extinct.

Why did dire wolves become extinct?

It could be that the prey they depended on for food died out. A change in climate could have played a part in their extinction. Also, many wolves died in tar pits. They may have gone after prey that was trapped in the pits and become stuck themselves.

How did people learn about dire wolves?

Many dire wolf fossils have been found. Thousands were dug up from a layer of asphalt that hardened beneath tar pits. Whole wolf skeletons have been built from the fossils. Because there is a big supply of fossils, the dire wolf has been studied a great deal.

Are any modern wolves like the dire wolf?

The dire wolf is often compared to the gray wolf that exists now. The dire wolf looked similar, but it was bigger. The dire wolf had a larger head and massive teeth. Its legs were shorter, however, than those of the gray wolf.

Think Link

1. Why do questions make good headings for research notes?

2. How do scientists know about wildlife that lived thousands of years ago?

3. What are some possible reasons why dire wolves became extinct?

Try It!

As you work on your investigation, think about how headings can be used to organize your information.

Genre

Realistic Fiction involves stories about people and events that are true to life and that could really happen.

Comprehension Strategy

⭐ **Making Connections** As you read, make connections between what you already know about habitats and what you are reading.

Two Days in May

by Harriet Peck Taylor
illustrated by Leyla Torres

Focus Questions
How do you think deer find their way into the city? What can be done to protect the deer in the city?

Read the story to find the meanings of these words, which are also in "Two Days in May":

✦ relocates
✦ cautiously
✦ appreciate
✦ sharp
✦ stranded
✦ detect
✦ exclaimed
✦ extended

Vocabulary Strategy

Context Clues are hints in the text. They help you find the meanings of words. Use context clues to find the meaning of *exclaimed*.

Vocabulary
Warm-Up

Tess clumped into the kitchen in sturdy boots. To her intelligent dog, Zip, the boots announced that Tess was going hiking. He wagged his tail eagerly. "Not today, boy," said Tess. "I'm going solo."

Tess had another roommate, Gwen. The two of them had adopted Zip from a group that relocates unwanted pets. He had grown attached to Tess quickly. "We'll take a walk later," Tess promised as she left.

Fog blurred the morning air. Cautiously, Tess made her way to the park. She latched her bike to a stand and headed for the hiking trails.

Tess liked to be out by herself. Today, however, she could appreciate the value of a hiking buddy. An extra set of sharp eyes might help in the fog.

Tess set off on a trail she knew well. Before long, however, she came to a place she did not recognize. As Tess turned to look around, her foot slipped into a hole. Tess's ankle twisted, and she fell to the ground. Now Tess was not only lost, but also badly hurt. She was stranded in the woods.

When Tess did not return, Gwen became worried. She put Zip in the car and drove to the park, where she saw Tess's bike still in the stand. Gwen let Zip out and said, "Go on, Zip! Find Tess!" She knew that the dog could detect Tess's scent.

Soon, Zip made his way to Tess. "Zip!" she exclaimed. "Thank you for finding me!" Tess extended her arms and hugged her furry friend.

GAME

Charades

Use the vocabulary words to play a game of charades with classmates. Choose one of the words to act out. The first person to correctly identify the word and explain its meaning will take the next turn as actor.

Concept Vocabulary

The concept word for this lesson is **protect.** To **protect** means "to keep something or someone safe." Talk about some ways wild animals protect themselves. Also discuss ways that people help protect wild animals.

Realistic Fiction involves stories about people and events that are true to life and that could really happen.

Comprehension Strategy

 Making Connections

As you read, make connections between what you already know about habitats and what you are reading.

Focus Questions

How do you think deer find their way into the city? What can be done to protect the deer in the city?

Two Days in May

by Harriet Peck Taylor

illustrated by Leyla Torres

Early one Saturday morning in May, I went to our fire escape window and rubbed the sleep from my eyes. I looked down at the small garden I had planted behind our apartment building. Five animals were grazing on the new lettuce in my garden!

"Mama! Mama!" I called. "Come see what's in our yard!"

Mama hurried over to the window and gasped. "Sonia, those animals are deer, but how did they get here?" she asked. "I'll run and tell Mr. Donovan."

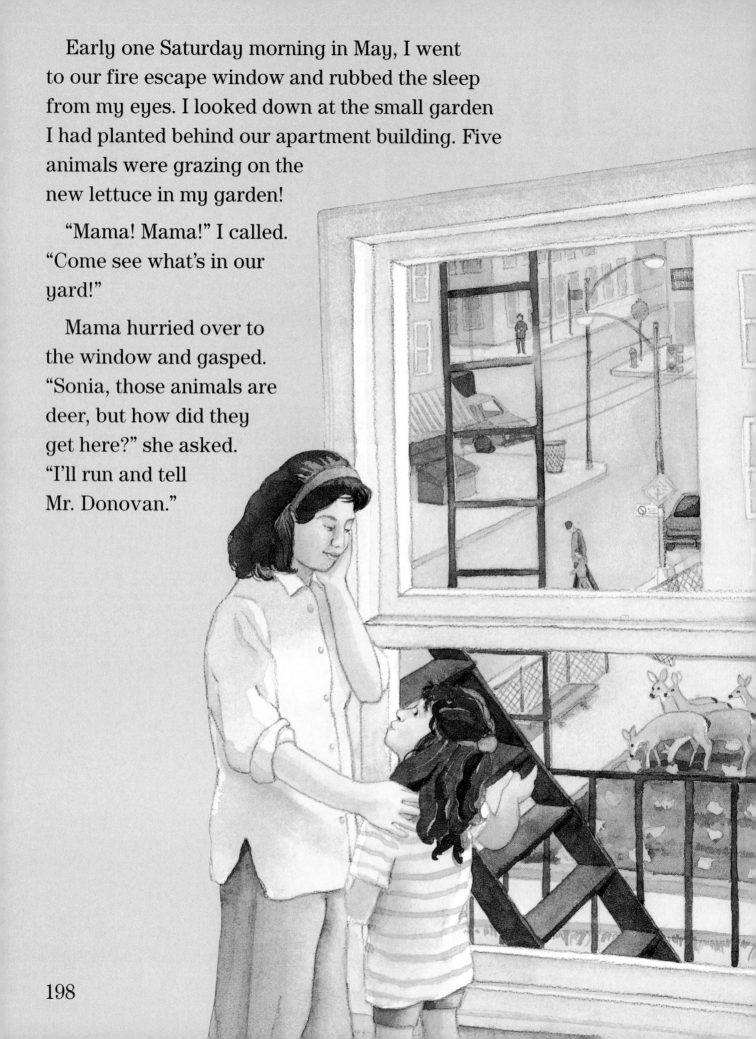

By the time Papa and I got out to the courtyard, a small crowd was gathering.

"Papa, why are there deer in the city?" I asked.

"The deer may have come all this way looking for food. They probably smelled your garden," he explained.

I thought I had never seen such an amazing sight. Their fur was a golden brown, and they balanced on tiny hooves. They had nervous tails, and eyes that were big and black and gentle.

Down the block a train rumbled by, but here life seemed to stand still. Pigeons and squirrels were almost the only birds or animals we ever saw in our neighborhood.

Looking around, I recognized many neighbors. There was Isidro Sánchez and his sister, Ana. Standing near me were Mr. Smiley, owner of Smiley's Laundromat, and my best friend, Peach, and Chester and Clarence Martin and the Yasamura sisters from down the hall. I saw Mr. Benny, the taxi driver, and the old Pigeon Lady, who was smiling brightly. I noticed that even neighbors who were almost strangers were standing close to each other and whispering in a friendly way. Well, everyone except Mr. Smiley and the Pigeon Lady, who were not on speaking terms. Mr. Smiley was angry because the Pigeon Lady fed her pigeons in front of his Laundromat, and he thought that was bad for business.

Mr. Donovan, our landlord, approached Papa. They spoke in hushed voices, but I was all ears.

"Luis, I, too, think the deer are really beautiful, but we both know they can't stay here," whispered Mr. Donovan. "They could be hit by a car. They belong in the woods, not in the city. I think we'd better call the animal control officers."

Papa nodded solemnly, and they walked off.

The Pigeon Lady came up to Peach and me and said, "Oh, girls, aren't they wonderful!"

"Yes!" we both answered together.

"I think two of the deer may be smaller. Those are probably females, or does. The males are called bucks. I used to see deer many years ago when I lived in the country."

Soon, Papa and Mr. Donovan returned with worried looks on their faces. They gathered the group together.

"The animal control office wants to shoot the deer," said Papa. "It's the law. The city is afraid the deer will starve."

"There aren't enough woods left for all the deer to find a home," added Mr. Donovan. "That's why the young deer wander far away. They're looking for territory of their own."

Everyone was so quiet that all you could hear was street sounds: honking and beeping, rumbling and humming.

Mr. Benny was the first to speak. "We can't let them shoot the deer. There must be another way."

"Yeah! That's right!" said Teresa Yasamura.

All around, people were nodding in agreement.

Then Chester spoke up. "They wouldn't shoot the deer in front of this many people. It would be too dangerous."

"It's true!" exclaimed Papa. "We can form a human wall around the deer without getting too close."

"Right on!" said Isidro. "We'll stay here until we can figure out what to do."

And that was the beginning of our peaceful protest.

Mr. Benny wrinkled his brow. "I remember reading a few months back about an organization that rescues and relocates animals that are stranded or injured. A fox had been hit by a car but wasn't badly hurt. This outfit took it in until it healed and then found a new home for it far from busy streets. I'll go see if I can find the number."

A little while later, Mr. Benny returned and announced, "The wildlife rescuer isn't in at the moment, but I left a message for him to call. I said it was an emergency."

When the animal control officer arrived, he saw the crowd surrounding the deer and decided not to take any chances. "If you don't mind, folks," he said, "I'll just hang around until you've all had enough and gone home." But we weren't leaving.

We stayed all afternoon, waiting anxiously, hoping to hear from the rescue organization. We got to know one another better, and we learned more about the deer.

Peach's eyes were wide and bright. "Look how they rotate their big soft ears to the left and right," she exclaimed.

Clarence said, "We studied deer in science. Their hearing is very sharp. It helps them detect enemies approaching from far away."

Mr. Benny nodded as he walked over to us. "I sometimes see this kind of deer at night, in the headlights, when I drive way past the city limits. When they're startled by the taxi's lights, their tails go up like flags. The tails are white underneath, which means the animals are white-tailed deer."

The deer grazed and slept cautiously, always alert to danger. They watched us with curious, intelligent eyes. I could see that the people made them uncomfortable, and it helped me appreciate that these really were wild animals. We tried to keep our distance and not make any sudden movements.

When evening came, the crowd grew. We talked quietly and told jokes as we kept watch over our silent friends. We ordered pizza from Giuseppe's.

Ana Sánchez spoke to the animal control officer. "Would you like a slice of pizza?" she asked.

"Thanks so much," he said. "My name is Steve Scully, and I understand how hard this must be for all of you. This is the part of my job I dislike.

"The problem is population growth. We've built towns and highways where there were once forests and streams. Now there is very little habitat left for the deer. There is no easy solution." He shook his head sadly.

I begged Papa to let me sleep outside all night, since almost everyone was staying. Mama came out with my baby brother, Danny. She brought blankets, a quilt, a jacket, and even my stuffed dog, Hershey.

Mama sat close and draped her arm across my shoulders. "Are you sure you'll be warm enough, Sonia?" she asked.

"I'm sure," I said.

We sat silently together, admiring the deer.

Finally she said, "I have to go put Danny to bed." She kissed me on the top of my head. "Sweet dreams, pumpkin."

I slept like a bear cub, curled in a ball against Papa's broad back.

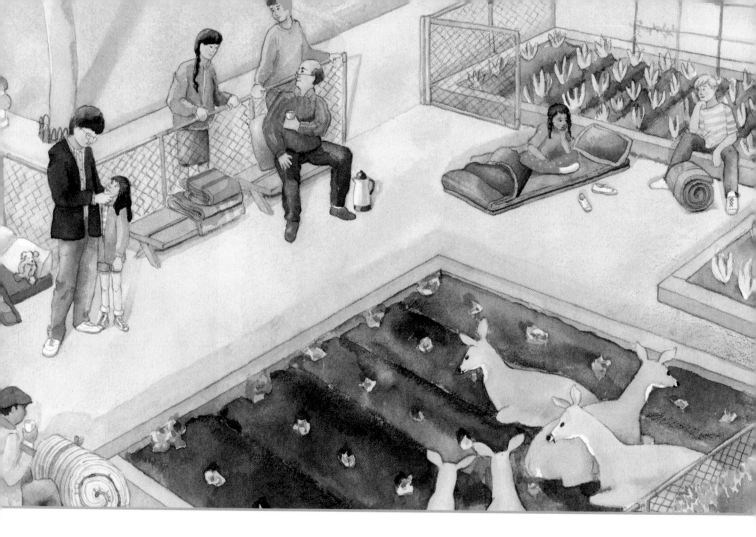

Next morning, I awoke with the sun in my eyes and city sounds buzzing in my ears. Papa hugged me and asked how I liked camping out.

"I dreamed I was sleeping with the deer in cool forests under tall trees."

"You were, Sonia!" he said, laughing. "But not in the forest."

I looked at the deer. "Has the wildlife rescuer called back?" I asked.

"Yes, Sonia. The organization called late last night and hopes to get someone out here this morning."

The group was quiet as we all continued to wait.

Later that morning, a rusty orange truck pulled up. The man who got out had a friendly, open face. All eyes were on him.

"Hi, folks. My name is Carl Jackson, and I'm with the wildlife rescue organization," he said. "I need to put the deer in crates in order to take them to our center. Don't be alarmed—I'm going to shoot them with a small amount of tranquilizer to make them sleep for a little while." Then, as they wobbled on unsteady legs, he grabbed them gently and guided them toward the wooden crates.

Carl turned to the crowd and smiled. "I'm an animal lover, too, and all of you should feel proud for helping save these deer. I'll find a home for them in the woods, where they'll be safe and happy and have plenty to eat."

Steve Scully came forward and extended his hand to Carl. "Glad you came, man."

A cheer went up from the crowd. People slapped each other on the back. Isidro high-fived everyone, including Mr. Donovan and the Pigeon Lady. Peach and I hugged each other, and Papa shook hands with Carl and Steve. I said goodbye to Teresa and Sandy Yasamura and to Mr. Benny.

I even saw Mr. Smiley shake the Pigeon Lady's hand. "Maybe you can feed the pigeons *behind* my Laundromat," he said. "I have a little space back there."

The Pigeon Lady smiled.

A few days later, Papa got a call from Carl. One
of the does had given birth to two fawns! And Carl
had found a home for all seven deer in a wooded
area northwest of the city.

Sometimes, when I'm sitting on the fire escape,
watching the flickering city lights, I think of the
deer. In my mind, they're gliding silently across
tall grass meadows all aglow in silver moonlight.

Meet the Author

Harriet Peck Taylor

Harriet Peck Taylor has loved two things her entire life: painting and nature. She also loves animals, both wild and tame. She once had a coyote follow her and her two dogs on a number of walks. Whether she is writing or walking in the woods, Taylor is careful to both enjoy and respect nature and its animals.

Meet the Illustrator

Leyla Torres

As a child in South America, Leyla Torres spent a lot of time making rag dolls, painting, or reading books. After college, she became involved with a group of puppeteers. Creating puppet shows inspired Torres to make books. Six years after moving to New York City and learning English, Torres completed her first book. She now lives in Vermont with her husband and enjoys painting in her workshop.

Animals and Their Habitats

Theme Connections

Within the Selection

1. Why would Sonia's garden in the city not make a good home for the deer?

2. "Two Days in May" is based on a true story. Why are more deer and other wildlife coming to the city?

Across Selections

3. How is this story like "Make Way for Ducklings"?

4. How is it different?

Beyond the Selection

5. What does "Two Days in May" tell you about animals and their habitats?

6. How can your community get involved to help animals in your neighborhood?

Write about It!

Describe how you or someone you know helped an animal in your neighborhood.

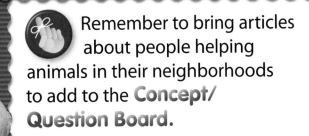

Remember to bring articles about people helping animals in their neighborhoods to add to the **Concept/ Question Board.**

Science Inquiry

A National Pleasure

Are you a nature lover? Then Yellowstone National Park is the place for you! No other park can match the array of wildlife and land features found here.

Many members of the deer family make their home at the park. Elk, moose, and deer are a common sight on the ranges. Bears, wolves, and many kinds of birds might also be seen and heard.

Hiking trails offer a chance to get close to nature. Guests can hike on their own or with a park ranger who will guide them. Will you be visiting in the winter when the ground may be covered with snow? No problem! You can strap on cross-country skis and hit the trails.

More outdoor adventures await you at Yellowstone. You can fish, boat, and bike. At the end of the day, pitch a tent at one of the campgrounds. Do you not like sleeping outdoors? Then relax in one of the cabins, lodges, or inns at the park.

No trip to the park would be complete without seeing Old Faithful. This is the most famous geyser in the world. The park boasts six grand geysers that spew steam and hot water more than one hundred feet into the air.

Do you want even more water features? Then you will **appreciate** the park's hot springs and waterfalls. Many of these spots can be reached or viewed from marked trails.

Water from rain, melted snow, and ice seeps miles into the earth, where it comes in contact with molten rock. The superheated water sprays out of the ground as steam and boiling water.

Don't delay! Make plans now to visit Yellowstone. *It's more than a park—it's a national pleasure.*

Think Link

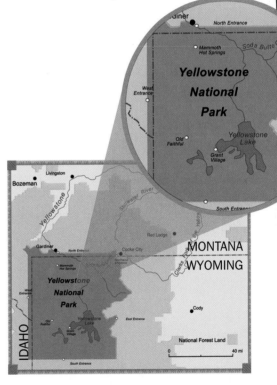

1. In what states is Yellowstone National Park located?

2. What is the purpose of the advertisement?

3. Matter has three forms: solid, liquid, and gas. Find examples of each in the advertisement above.

Try It!

As you work on your investigation, think about how you can use a map to show information in your final presentation.

Read the article to find the meanings of these words, which are also in "Crinkleroot's Guide to Knowing Animal Habitats":

✦ patch
✦ rich
✦ habitats
✦ variety
✦ recognize
✦ prey
✦ migrating
✦ vast

Vocabulary Strategy

Context Clues are hints in the text. They help you find the meanings of words. Use context clues to find the meaning of *prey*.

Vocabulary
Warm-Up

A swamp is a shallow wetland where trees grow. Some swamps have fresh water. Some contain salt water. A mangrove swamp has both. It is a patch of wetland that is close to an ocean.

Mangrove trees grow in mud that is rich in salt but poor in oxygen. Few trees can survive in this setting. Salt kills most plants. Soil that is always soft and moist does not support a tree.

Mangroves are special trees. They are able to filter out the salt in the soil and water. Their long, tangled roots prop them up. The roots look like they have been unearthed. They rise out of the water to take in the air they need.

Mangrove trees provide habitats for a variety of wildlife. Birds build nests in the trees. These include egrets, herons, and pelicans. In a mangrove tree, the birds find a home and a ready source of food as well.

The birds wade in the mangrove swamp. They look for fish that swim among the roots of the trees. The birds are quickly able to recognize and seize their prey. A heron grabs fish with its sharp beak. A pelican dives underwater and scoops fish in its pouch.

Some small fish stay safe in the shelter of the mangrove roots. They feed on crabs, shrimp, and worms. Then, when they are grown, they leave. These migrating fish move from the swamp to the vast waters of the ocean.

GAME

Writing Sentences

Use each vocabulary word in two sentences. First, use the word in a sentence that asks a question. Then use the word in a sentence that is a statement. Write your sentences on a sheet of paper.

Concept Vocabulary

The concept word for this lesson is *ecosystem.* An **ecosystem** is a group of living things and the environment in which they live. A desert and a rain forest are examples of ecosystems. What kinds of animals live in different ecosystems? What helps these animals survive in their environments?

Crinkleroot's Animal

Guide to Knowing Habitats

by Jim Arnosky

Focus Questions

What would it be like to study animal habitats as a job? Why is it important to learn about and to protect different animal habitats?

Hello! My name is Crinkleroot. I'm an explorer and a wildlife finder. I've found so many wild creatures sharing this sweet earth, I lost count somewhere around a billion!

I see so many wild critters because I know where they all live. The natural places where wild animals live are called habitats.

I'm going to visit lots of different wildlife habitats. You can come too!

The three things wildlife
need to survive are:

FOOD,

COVER,
(hiding places),

and WATER.

Find all three,
and you will
find wildlife.

The first place I want to show you is a watery place, or wetland.

CROSS SECTION OF A WETLAND:
mud
water table (water level in soil)
sand, pebbles, and stones.

222

A wetland is any place where water is near, at, or just above the surface of the ground. You may have a tiny wetland in your own backyard where the soil is always moist and the grass grows more lush.

NOTE: Some types of wetlands are not firm enough to walk on. The best way to observe most wetlands is in the company of an adult and from the safety of higher ground or a sturdy boardwalk.

The three most common wetlands are marshes, swamps, and bogs. A marsh is full of tall grasses, cattails, and reeds. Here water is above ground in many spots.

Canada geese

great blue heron

mergansers

painted turtle

red-winged blackbird

mallards

bullfrog

muskrat

A swamp is a place where many woody plants grow and water covers nearly all the land.

egret

anhinga

otter

alligator

mud turtle

little blue heron

water moccasin

A bog is a place where the land actually floats on water.

moose

The shallow water of any wetland is a world of plants, rocks, sand, and sunken trees.

sunfish

newt

damselfly larva

freshwater mussel

water boatman

crayfish

minnows

dragonfly larva

madtom

It is a rich weedy habitat for underwater wildlife.

pickerel

snapping turtle

227

In a woodland, tree trunks, stems, and branches criss-cross and overlap. It takes sharp eyes to pick out even the noisiest creatures, like hammering woodpeckers or chirping red squirrels. But make no mistake! Any woodland is habitat for a variety of wildlife. For every animal you hear or see, there are many more hiding.

two moths, red squirrel, deer, inchworm, box turtle, spider, five honeybees, two chickadees, fawn, chipmunk, wood thrush, woodpecker, bark beetle, skunk, oak worm (caterpillar), brown creeper, two bats

In the woods, animals may be living high in the treetops, in middle branches or trunks, or on the woodland floor.

See if you can find the wildlife living in this little patch of woods. (I'll give you a hint: there are twenty-four in all. Twenty-seven if you count walking stick, Sassafrass, and me.)

Climb aboard my old jalopy! There are some interesting places I want to show you that are miles apart. Along the way, we're sure to spot some wildlife near the road.

crows

ring-necked pheasant

deer

woodchuck

230

Rabbits, deer, woodchucks, and other normally shy animals come out to the roadsides to feed on lush green plants growing in the open sunlight.

Roadsides are also hunting grounds for hungry crows, hawks, and kestrels.

red-tailed hawk

kestrel

35 MPH

NATURE

rabbit

231

Our first stop is a farmer's cornfield. Cornfields provide an ever-changing habitat for wildlife. In the spring gulls, swallows, and bluebirds feed on beetles, grubs, and earthworms unearthed by the farmer's plow.

By midsummer, when the corn stalks have grown high enough to provide cover, small animals move in to nest and raise their young.

At ripening time the cornfield becomes a supermarket for raiding raccoons.

By late fall, after the field of corn has been freshly cut and harvested, the scattered kernels are a feast for migrating geese.

burrowing owl

prairie dogs

Most small grassland animals are birds or burrowers—or both!

From small hillside meadows to vast rolling plains, grasslands are wide open spaces where wildlife can thrive.

goldfinch

monarch butterfly

tick

When walking in grassland, stop to check your clothes for ticks. Ticks are numerous in tall grass.

You'll find more kinds of insects and spiders in grasslands than in any other habitat.

pronghorn antelope

bison

The largest inhabitants of grasslands are grazing animals.

At first, grassland looks void of anything but waving green stems. But take time to really look and you will discover something wonderful.

The badger is a grassland predator that can dig down twelve feet to catch burrowing prey.

The coyote and red fox are open country predators that often share the same hunting grounds.

vole

spider

grasshopper

woodchuck

235

vulture

Wherever the road leads, you will find wildlife living there. Even the hottest, driest places can be home to animals. In the drylands, wildlife find cover behind sage brush and cactus, beneath rock ledges, or for some, simply by digging in and covering up with sand. Succulent plants provide both food and water. And for predators, there is prey.

236

Here is a sampling of the many wildlife species that inhabit drylands from sage brush country to desert sands.

mule deer

armadillo

kangaroo rat

jackrabbit

diamondback rattlesnake

roadrunner

collared lizard

broad-billed hummingbird

horned lizard

elf owl

raven

MUSTLPAST

NATURE

pika

Learn to recognize the different wildlife habitats, from lowlands to mountains, wetlands to drylands. Don't be fooled by how small a place may be. Some wild critters get by in surprisingly little space—a bit of brush, a swampy puddle, a pile of rocks, a tiny woodlot, or a lone cactus.

Well now! I told you we'd cover a lot of territory and we did! I counted over eighty different wildlife species on our trip. How many did you count? I hope you enjoyed the journey. I did. So did Sassafrass. She always likes riding in the old jalopy. We'll see you soon. Until then, remember, wherever you go, you share the world with wildlife.

bighorn
sheep

Meet the Author and Illustrator

Jim Arnosky

Like his character Crinkleroot, Jim Arnosky loves to travel and explore new places. The details of the natural world fascinate him. When he travels, Arnosky takes pictures and notes to help him remember everything he sees. He then uses what he learns to write and illustrate his books. Arnosky's home is a farm in Vermont, where he likes to raise sheep and play his guitar.

Animals and Their Habitats

Theme Connections

Within the Selection

1. Where does Crinkleroot look to find wildlife?
2. How many different species of wildlife did you count on this journey?

Across Selections

3. How is this selection like "One Small Place in a Tree"?
4. How is it different?

Beyond the Selection

5. What lessons have you learned about animals and their habitats?
6. What does Crinkleroot mean when he says, " . . . wherever you go, you share the world with wildlife"?

Write about It!

Describe a habitat you visited away from your neighborhood.

Remember to think of questions about different animal habitats to add to the **Concept/Question Board.**

Science Inquiry

Deserts Are Not Deserted

What do you think of when you hear the word desert? Do you picture a blazing sun and vast stretch of sand? That is one type of desert. Did you know a desert can also be cold? Some deserts are covered with snow and ice. The arctic tundra is a cold desert.

Both kinds of deserts are dry. A hot desert gets just 4 to 20 inches of rain per year. A cold desert gets that amount of snow in a year. The lack of water in a desert affects life there. Only certain kinds of plants and animals can survive.

Animals in a hot desert must find shelter from the sun. Insects will move around a twig or leaf to stay in its shade. Mice burrow beneath the sand. They come out at night, when the air is cooler.

Animals in a cold desert must deal with an extreme climate too. Squirrels hibernate for the coldest months. Migrating birds, such as the tern, stay alive by flying to warmer climates in August. In May they return to the tundra.

Animals' bodies help them adapt to desert life. Rabbits in a hot desert have large ears. Their ears give off heat, which helps them cool down. Camels have long eyelashes that keep sand out of their eyes. Musk oxen and polar bears have a lot of body fat. They also have thick fur. The fat and fur help keep them warm in the cold tundra.

A desert might seem like an empty place, but life does exist there. You just might have to look harder to find it.

Desert Life

Hot Desert
- animals seek protection from sun
- animals' bodies give off heat
- few large mammals live here

- dry weather
- animals adapt to extreme conditions
- animals are more active at certain times

Cold Desert
- animals seek protection from cold
- animals' bodies hold in heat
- reptiles do not live here

Think Link

1. How can animals adapt to live in hot deserts?

2. How can animals adapt to live in cold deserts?

3. What does the middle section of the Venn diagram show?

Try It!

As you work on your investigation, try using a Venn diagram to compare and contrast information.

What special qualities do animals have
to help them survive in their habitats? How might we
be a danger to some animals if we are not careful?
How can we help?

from
If Not for the Cat

a book of haiku poems | by Jack Prelutsky
| *illustrated by Ted Rand*

We are we are we
Are we are we are we are
Many in our hill.

Focus Questions What might be happening in an animal habitat when we are not looking? What do wild animals do where you live? How long have they been doing those things?

Behind the Redwood Curtain

by Natasha Wing

illustrated by Lori Anzalone

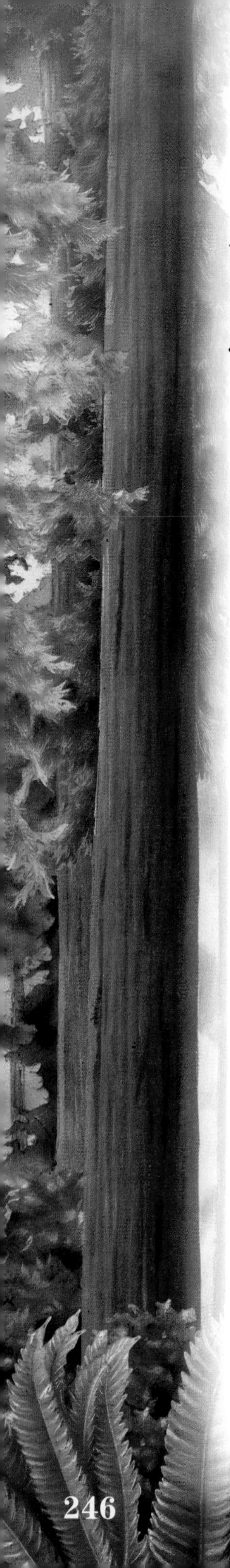

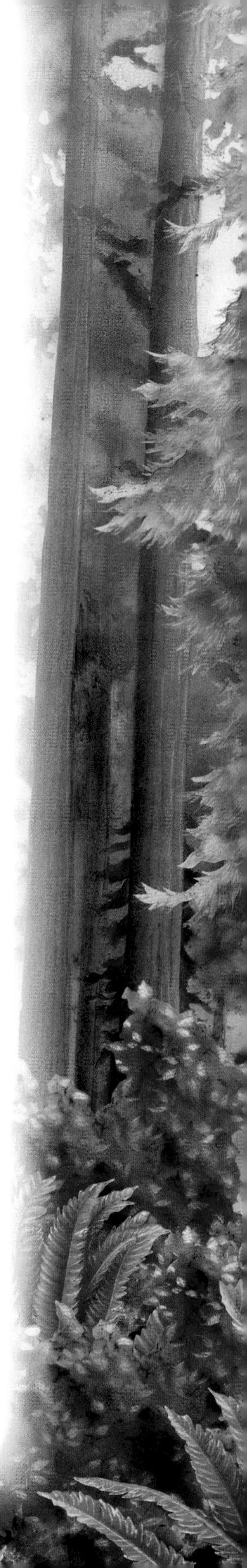

Redwood trees rise like skyscrapers
Fingering the clouds in search of moisture
Pulling down the fog and passing it
From limb to limb
Into the deep of the forest.
The fog blankets the forest
Blocking out light, movement, and sound
Like a curtain
Draped across a stage.
Yet behind the redwood curtain
Black bear walk and stalk their prey
Deer sleep and leap away
Slugs climb and slime on leaves
Birds sing and wing in the breeze.
The show must go on
As it has for thousands of years
Behind the redwood curtain.

Test Prep

Identifying and Using Important Words

Each question or answer choice has important words. These words will help you answer the question correctly.

Read this item to yourself. Think about the important words in the question and answer choices.

According to this article, what should you do with a garden in the fall?

(A) Use less water.

(B) Use more fertilizer.

(C) Pull all the plants out of the ground.

(D) Cover the plants with plastic.

Important words in the question are *According to this article.* They tell you that you should use the information in the article, not other things that you might have heard or read. Another important word is *fall.* It tells you the time of year to think about. In the answer choices, some of the important words are *less*, *more*, and *all.* Even small words can help you understand the question and answer choices.

Test-Taking Practice

Read the selection "The Starling." Then answer numbers 1 through 4.

A bird that almost everyone knows is the starling. Most people think the starling is an American bird. It is not. A few dozen starlings were brought here from Europe more than a hundred years ago. They must have liked it. Now they are found all over the United States. There are millions of them.

Starlings are mostly black. They are about six inches long. Their feathers sometimes seem to change colors. You might see a little green or purple when the light shines on them.

Here is something strange about starlings. In the summer, the beak of a starling is yellow. In the winter, it is black.

You probably will not see just one or two starlings at a time. That is because starlings like to live in flocks of many birds. You will know when a flock of starlings is nearby. They will make a lot of noise. A flock of starlings can have more than one hundred birds.

GO ON

Some birds have beautiful songs. The songs always sound the same. People often know a bird by its song. This is not true about starlings. They can make many different sounds. They try to sound like other birds. In a city, starlings might even try to make sounds like horns honking.

Starlings are also very hungry birds. They eat seeds, berries, and bugs. Starlings do something that is not very nice. They eat so much that there is no food for other birds. When starlings come to an area, they often chase away other birds.

Just like other birds, starlings like to keep their babies safe. They make nests of sticks, feathers, and even trash. Starlings can live in trees and also buildings. Starlings sometimes make their nests in a person's house. Can you imagine waking up and finding a starling flying in your bedroom?

GO ON

Use what you learned from "The Starling" to answer Numbers 1 through 4. Write your answers on a piece of paper.

1. To learn more about starlings, you should

  Ⓐ look in a dictionary under "birds."

  Ⓑ look in an encyclopedia.

  Ⓒ ask a friend who has a big yard.

  Ⓓ find a book about pet birds.

2. Starlings are different from other birds because starlings

  Ⓐ sometimes sound like horns honking.

  Ⓑ build nests to keep their babies safe.

  Ⓒ live all over the United States.

  Ⓓ eat seeds, berries, and bugs.

3. What is the author's main purpose for writing "The Starling"?

  Ⓐ To tell why starlings are noisy

  Ⓑ To prove that starlings are beautiful

  Ⓒ To encourage people to feed starlings

  Ⓓ To share interesting facts about starlings

4. Why is it a problem that starlings are very hungry birds?

  Ⓐ It is not good for starlings to eat trash.

  Ⓑ Starlings eat food that people need.

  Ⓒ There is no food left for other birds.

  Ⓓ The starlings get fat and cannot fly.

Unit 3

Money

What do you think of when you hear the word *money?* Maybe you think of the new bike or video game you want. Perhaps you think about getting a summer job and how much money you would like to make. Have you ever thought about how money works? What role has money played in peoples' lives, both in the past and in the present? What creative ideas have people had to earn money? Let's find out!

Fine Art
Theme Connection

Look at the painting *Market Day* by Richard H. Fox. What are people buying and selling? How is this market similar to a shopping mall? How is it different?

Richard H. Fox (b. 1960/American).
Market Day. 2005.

Oil on Canvas.

252

BIG
Idea

What is the value
of money?

Read the article to find the meanings of these words, which are also in "It's a Deal!":

✦ ancient
✦ valuable
✦ traders
✦ kingdom
✦ solution
✦ deal
✦ forms
✦ eventually

Vocabulary Strategy

Word Structure is when parts of a word help you understand the word's meaning. Use word structure to find the meaning of *valuable*.

Vocabulary
Warm-Up

The Silk Road was an ancient trade route that joined East and West. It stretched more than six thousand miles from Asia to Europe. The Silk Road got its name from one of China's most valuable products: silk.

Few traders traveled the full length of the Silk Road. The route was too long. There was bound to be trouble along the way. Wars and bandits made the course risky in spots. In some places, outsiders were not trusted. Some kings would not let foreign traders pass through their kingdom.

Traders came up with a solution. They set up staging points on the Silk Road. They loaded their goods at one

point. Then they traveled to another post. There, they would pass the load on to the next team of drivers.

Traders from the East carried silk, jade, and spices. Gems, gold, and perfume came from the West. People were eager to have treasures from far-off lands. They hoped to work out a fair deal. Traders tried to judge each other's honesty before they swapped goods.

More than goods moved back and forth on the Silk Road. Ideas from distant lands were exchanged too. People began to learn about new forms of art. They heard new languages. Knowledge about science was passed along.

Eventually, the staging points grew into towns. Traders built homes and set up shops. Some of those cities on the old Silk Road thrive to this day.

GAME

Write a Riddle

Make up a riddle for each of the vocabulary words. For example, for the word *ancient,* you might write "I have been around for a very long time." Exchange papers with a classmate, and solve each other's riddles.

Concept Vocabulary

The concept word for this lesson is **worth.** An item's **worth** is the money that someone is willing to pay for it. How does the worth of an item that is easy to get compare to the worth of an item that is hard to get? Discuss your ideas with classmates.

Expository Text is nonfiction that is written to inform, to explain, or to persuade.

Comprehension Strategy

⭐ **Clarifying**
As you read, make a note of sections you do not understand and reread them to better understand what they say.

IT'S A DEAL!

by Catherine Ripley

illustrated by R. W. Alley

It's a deal.

Focus Questions

What would it be like to have to barter for everything you need rather than use money? If you could design your own money, what would it look like?

257

You've had your eye on Jerry's red fire truck for days. He never plays with it, so you ask if you can have it.

"Hmm," he says. "What will you give me for it?"

"My bag of marbles."

"It's a deal!"

You have just bought Jerry's truck by using an ancient system called barter. Barter is when you trade one thing for another instead of using money.

But wait—what if Jerry hadn't wanted your marbles?

That was a problem for people who traded things thousands of years ago, too. If no one wanted what you had to trade, you were out of luck. Over the years, traders figured out what people in their part of the world always seemed to want. In some places, you were sure of making a trade if you had a cow. In other places, it was better if you had a reindeer—or some butter, sheep, whales' teeth, corn, elephants, hoes, tea, shells, or salt. These were all early types of money.

But there were still problems.

Cowrie shells

People needed something better to barter. After a while, they started using valuable metals to trade. Everybody likes gold and silver and copper!

An ancient Egyptian wall painting of metalworkers weighing gold

When people first started bartering with metal, they used bars and chunks of all different sizes. The heavier your piece of metal, the more you could buy. This meant new problems. People had to weigh their pieces of metal every time they wanted to buy something.

What a nuisance! This is taking forever.

There must be a better way to buy a loaf of bread.

How do I know her scale works? What if she cheated and it's not all gold?

A pound of solid gold. I weighed it myself.

Sometimes traders marked their metal ahead of time to show how much each piece weighed—but there were problems with that way of doing things, too.

Finally people in a country called Lydia figured out a solution. Almost three thousand years ago, they stamped their king's special mark, a lion's head, on each piece of metal used for money in the kingdom. The lion's head was the king's promise that each piece was worth exactly what it was supposed to be worth. Since the kings of Lydia had always been known for their honesty, people everywhere trusted their stamps.

A coin from Lydia

Soon lots of countries were making their own stamped coins. But eventually people got tired of carrying around all that metal. More problems!

So traders started carrying notes that promised they had enough coins at home to buy the goods they wanted. These notes were the earliest forms of the paper money we use today.

Early coins from around the world

Early paper money from China

Coins and paper money
from around the world

Money has changed a lot since the people of
Lydia stamped coins with the royal lion's head. But
the idea is still the same. To get exactly what you
want from someone else, you still need to hand
over something of yours—whether it's a whale's
tooth, a bag of marbles, or a quarter. Only then
can you say, "It's a deal!"

Meet the Author

Catherine Ripley

Writing was Catherine Ripley's favorite activity in elementary school. Since then, she has been writing all the time. She has worked as an editor for the Canadian children's magazines *Cricket* and *Chickadee*. She enjoys adding mazes, puzzles, and games to her work. Most of all, she enjoys making words "dance . . . sparkle . . . live forever!"

Meet the Illustrator

R. W. Alley

Alley has drawn pictures for many stories, including the Paddington Bear books by Michael Bond. "I always imagine I'm the character that I'm drawing at the moment," says Alley. "I make faces and walk around. I try to be inside the drawing." Alley loves being an illustrator. "It's a good feeling to do something that makes people happy," he says.

Money

Theme Connections

Within the Selection

1. If you traded goods with friends, what items would have the best trade values?

2. If you could design a coin for your city or town, what would it show?

Beyond the Selection

3. People trade goods and services. What favor have you done for someone, and what favor did you receive in return?

4. How else do people pay for things that they want?

Write about It!

Describe a trade you have made or would like to make.

Remember to find pictures of coins or paper money to add to the **Concept/Question Board.**

Good as Gold

The California Gold Rush drew people to the West to seek their fortunes. Some believed mining was a quick way to become rich. Many people who flocked west did get rich. However, those who profited the most were not miners. They were people who provided goods and services. Here is what a journal entry might have looked like from a woman who traveled west with her husband.

Oct. 29, 1849

It has been four months today since we arrived in Sutter Creek. I am still missing home, but we have made a very good living here. James gave up mining last week. He said his time would be better spent helping me, and I didn't argue.

We have been selling at least 50 pies a day. It seems more hungry miners show up all the time. Fruit pies go for a dollar, and I get a dollar and a half for the meat pies. Even with the fee I pay to Mrs. Cress for her help, I am making a nice wage.

James and I plan to offer a laundry service too. With profits from the pies, we'll buy a couple of tubs, washboards, and some good soap. He says men are paying up to $8.00 for a batch of clean clothes. That's a deal I will take in a minute!

It's a strange thing. I would not have guessed a warm pie and a clean shirt were so valuable. I guess that, when miners come down from their rough camps, they want some comforts of home. Seems these things are good as gold.

Think Link

1. How were the woman and her husband able to expand their business?

2. Look at the abbreviations in the date and in the second paragraph of the journal entry. What kind of punctuation is used?

3. Why is the woman surprised that she can make money by selling pies and washing clothes?

Try It!

As you work on your investigation, look for words that you can abbreviate.

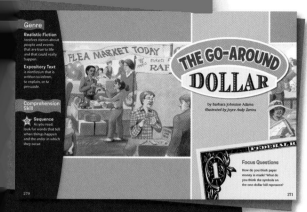

Read the story to find the meanings of these words, which are also in "The Go-Around Dollar":

- ✦ portrait
- ✦ inspect
- ✦ seal
- ✦ formula
- ✦ debts
- ✦ remains
- ✦ emblem
- ✦ counterfeit

Vocabulary Strategy

Apposition is when a word or group of words define another word in the same sentence. Use apposition to find the meaning of *portrait*.

Vocabulary

Warm-Up

The Wolves were in the playoffs! Tyler was a big fan of the local baseball team. Their portrait, a picture of the team, hung above his bed. Tyler would inspect the poster each day. He memorized the players' numbers. He even studied their league seal.

The Wolves had not done well the past few years. However, this season they had found a formula for success. Tyler had to see the game in person. Tickets were not cheap, so he set to work. Tyler did extra chores at home. He did odd jobs for neighbors. He even collected on his friends' debts. Ming-Da owed him two dollars; Connor owed four.

At last, Tyler had enough money. He walked to the ticket office. A block from the office, a sign caught Tyler's eye. It said, "Discount Playoff Tickets!! Buy Now!!" A young man stood by the sign. Tickets fanned out in his hand.

Tyler thought, *If I save money on the ticket, I can buy a souvenir with what remains of the cash.* Just then, a woman and two guards rushed up. The young man dropped the tickets and took off running. "What's going on?" Tyler asked.

Tyler recognized the emblem on the sleeve of the woman's jacket. She explained that she was an official with the Wolves organization. "These tickets are counterfeit. You're lucky you didn't waste your money. Why don't we show you where to buy a ticket that will get you into the game!"

GAME

Flash Cards

Make a set of flash cards with the vocabulary words. Write the word on one side and its definition on the other side. Use the flash cards to review the vocabulary words and definitions. Then ask a classmate to use the cards to quiz you.

Concept Vocabulary

The concept word for this lesson is *currency.* **Currency** is money—coins and paper—that people use. Instead of keeping all of their money with them in currency, many people put their money in a bank. They might have a checking account or a savings account. Why do you think people keep some of their money in bank accounts?

Genre

Realistic Fiction involves stories about people and events that are true to life and that could really happen.

Expository Text is nonfiction that is written to inform, to explain, or to persuade.

Comprehension Skill

★ **Sequence** As you read, look for words that tell when things happen and the order in which they occur.

THE GO-AROUND
DOLLAR

by Barbara Johnston Adams

illustrated by Joyce Audy Zarins

Focus Questions

How do you think paper money is made? What do you think the symbols on the one-dollar bill represent?

271

Every dollar travels from person to person in a different way. But each dollar starts out in the same place—the Bureau of Engraving and Printing in Washington, D.C. Since 1862, this is where our nation's paper money has been produced. The Bureau is part of the United States Treasury Department. At the Bureau, huge printing presses run around the clock, turning out dollar bills. In twenty-four hours, ten million one-dollar bills can be printed.

Dollars are printed in big sheets of thirty-two bills. First the basic design is printed. Then the sheets are cut in half and go back to the presses for an overprinting. This second printing adds information such as the serial numbers and the Treasury seal.

As bills are made, they're checked by people and machines over and over again to make sure they are perfect.

Finally, the sheets are cut into stacks of individual bills called bricks. Bricks are sent to one of twelve banks, located in different parts of the United States, called Federal Reserve Banks.

Federal Reserve Banks, in turn, send dollars to banks in cities, small towns, and neighborhoods. From here, dollars go into circulation, to be used by people all over America: in stores, cafeterias, movie theaters, and thousands of other places—wherever money changes hands. Here's what might have happened to one dollar. . . .

FEDERAL RESERVE NOTE

THE UNITED STATES OF AMERICA

The United States government has laws about the way dollar bills can be shown. For instance, a dollar drawn as an illustration for a book must be in black and white, not in full color. A dollar must also be shown either larger than one and one-half times the size of a real dollar, or smaller than three-quarters the size of a real dollar.

As Matt and Eric were walking
home from school one day . . .

A portrait of George Washington,
first president of the United
States, is on the front of every
one-dollar bill. Only people who
are no longer alive can have their
pictures on American money.

"What's that?"

"Wow! It's a dollar bill!"

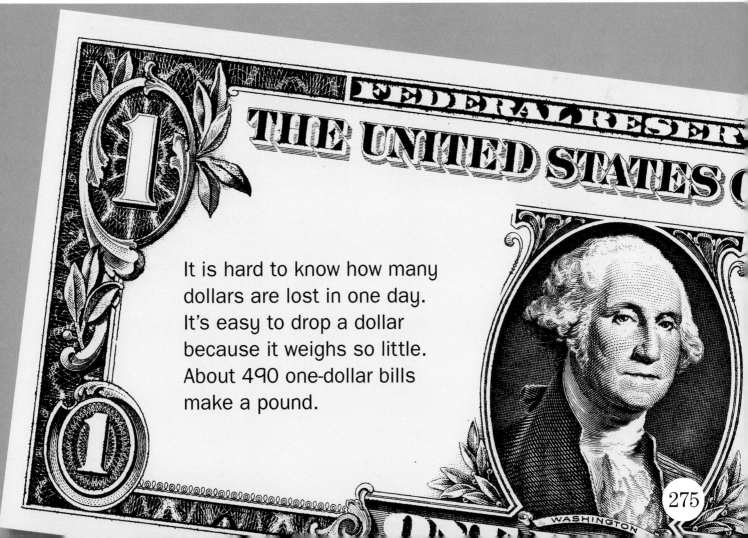

It is hard to know how many dollars are lost in one day. It's easy to drop a dollar because it weighs so little. About 490 one-dollar bills make a pound.

Matt offered to buy Eric's shoelaces for the dollar.

"Do they really glow in the dark?"

Dollar bills are used to buy things, pay back money that was borrowed, or pay for a service, such as a bus ride. There is a notice on each dollar that makes this clear: "This note is legal tender for all debts, public and private."

The front of every dollar has a long number in green ink, which appears in two different places. This is called the serial number. No two dollars have the same serial number. If a dollar is damaged while it is printed, it is replaced by a bill with a star where the last letter of the serial number would usually be. These bills are called star notes.

"Don't forget your change!"

. . . and Jennifer received the dollar as part of
her change from a five-dollar bill.

"Mom! Have you seen my jeans?"

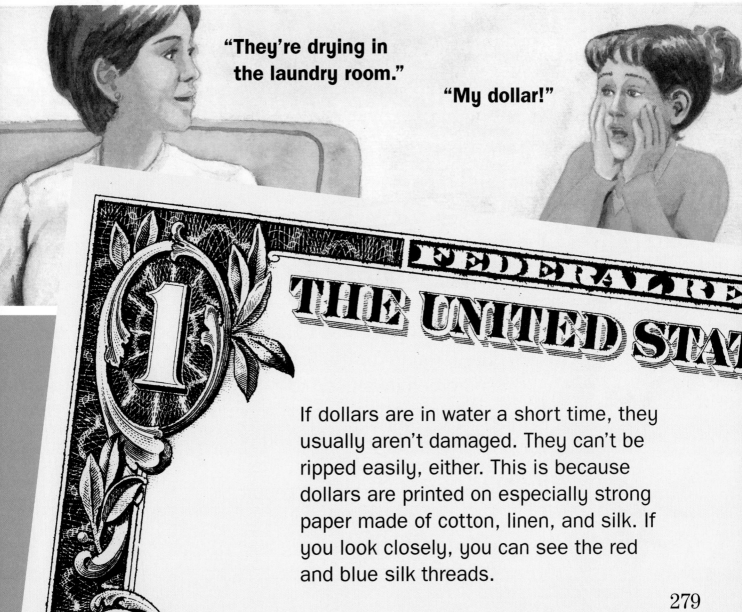

"They're drying in the laundry room."

"My dollar!"

If dollars are in water a short time, they usually aren't damaged. They can't be ripped easily, either. This is because dollars are printed on especially strong paper made of cotton, linen, and silk. If you look closely, you can see the red and blue silk threads.

Jennifer went to a flea market and bought a funny hat from Rob with the dollar. At a booth near Rob's, a ticket seller was handed an odd-looking dollar bill.

The formula for the black and green inks used to print dollars is a secret known only by the Bureau of Engraving and Printing. The secret is important; it keeps people from making fake, or counterfeit, bills exactly like the real ones.

Sometimes people called counterfeiters *do* make fake money. But it's very hard to make a dollar that looks and feels like a real one. When counterfeiters are caught, they're fined and sent to jail.

Back at home, Rob asked his sister
Kathy to do a chore for him. . . .

When a dollar changes hands, many people don't realize they're holding the Great Seal of the United States. The two sides of the Seal, an official symbol of our country, are shown in circles on the back of every one-dollar bill. One circle has an eagle in it; the other, a pyramid with an eye. The bald eagle, our national emblem, is holding arrows and an olive branch. The arrows stand for war and the olive branch for peace. The eagle faces the olive branch, which means the United States wants peace, not war. The pyramid stands for strength and growth; the eye, spiritual values.

"Come back here, Biscuit!"

Sometimes dollars are accidentally burned, chewed by animals, or torn. The Treasury Department will replace a bill if more than half of the original remains. If less than half remains, a government official must inspect the dollar before replacing it.

Lots of people say they see pictures of tiny owls or spiders near the corners of dollar bills. But the Bureau of Engraving and Printing says there are no such creatures on our money.

Kathy thought about different ways to spend the dollar.

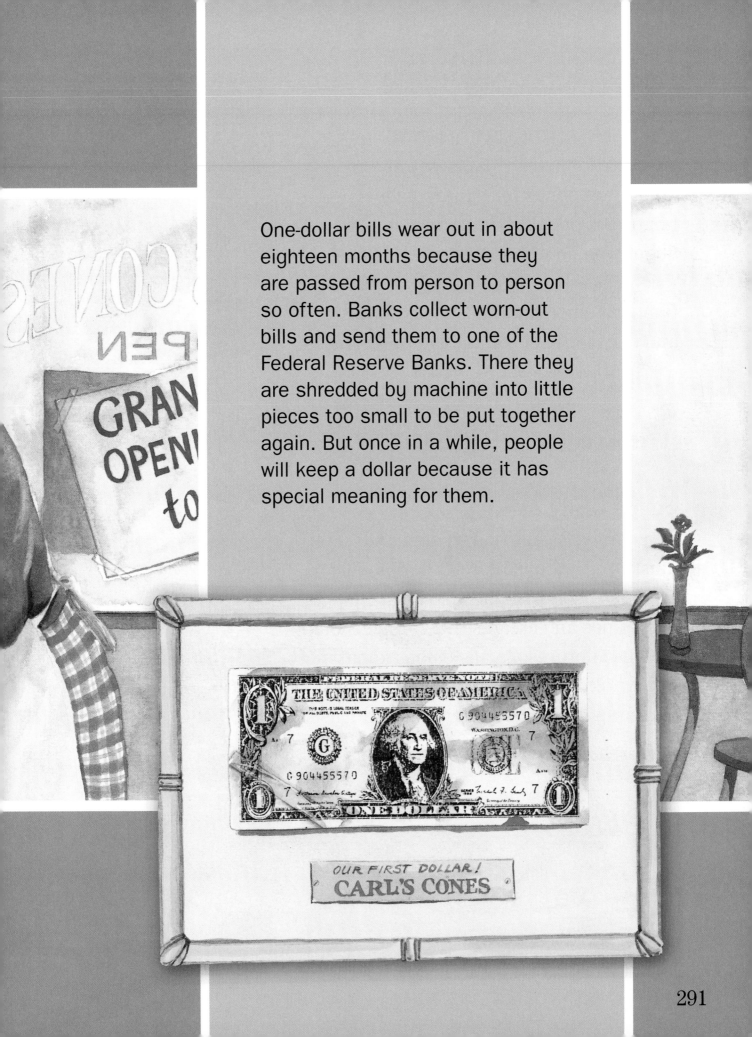

One-dollar bills wear out in about eighteen months because they are passed from person to person so often. Banks collect worn-out bills and send them to one of the Federal Reserve Banks. There they are shredded by machine into little pieces too small to be put together again. But once in a while, people will keep a dollar because it has special meaning for them.

OUR FIRST DOLLAR!
CARL'S CONES

Meet the Author

Barbara Johnston Adams

Barbara Johnston Adams writes nonfiction books for children about important people. She wrote a book about women who have won the Nobel Prize. She even wrote a book about the famous comedian, Bill Cosby. Adams and her family currently live in Virginia.

Meet the Illustrator

Joyce Audy Zarins

Joyce Audy Zarins has written and illustrated many children's books, such as *Toasted Bagels*. She also illustrates for magazines and creates three-dimensional metal sculptures. Zarins enjoys kayaking, hiking, skiing, and beach strolling. She currently lives and works in Massachusetts.

Money

Theme Connections

Within the Selection

1. What would you do if you found a dollar bill?
2. What are some things you could buy with one dollar?

Across Selections

3. How is the dollar bill in "The Go-Around Dollar" like the tree in "One Small Place in a Tree"?
4. How are the dollar bills we use like the early coins described in "It's a Deal!"?

Beyond the Selection

5. What famous person do you think should be pictured on American money? Explain why.
6. Why is it against the law for people to print their own money?

Write about It!

Create a time line that tells how one of your dollar bills was passed from person to person.

Remember to bring pictures of things you could buy with one dollar to add to the **Concept/Question Board**.

Children Cherish Chance to Learn

The book *We Need to Go to School* is a collection of true stories about childhood lost—almost. The tales come from children in Nepal. They had all been forced to work in carpet mills.

Author Tanya Roberts-Davis went to Nepal when she was just 16 years old. She hoped to point out the plight of child workers there. She stayed with children who had worked weaving rugs. Roberts-Davis gathered their poems and drawings. She recorded their stories.

The kids spoke of their poor families. They told of being sent to work at a young age. They had to help pay family costs and debts. Most of them never saw the money they worked so hard to earn.

A group called Rugmark changed life for these kids. Rugmark seeks to put an end to child labor.

The Rugmark label certifies that no child labor was used in making the rug.

They inspect factories like the rug mills in Nepal. When they find a child working, they try to help.

Each child in the book recalls the day he or she met a Rugmark official. The children were asked, "Do you want to go to school?" The answer was always "Yes!"

Rugmark centers offer these kids proper meals and homes. The children have time to play. They also have a chance to learn.

The children speak of their studies with pride. They know that education is the key to a bright future for them. Some plan to become doctors. Some want to be social workers.

The children's tales are sad, yet full of hope. They also carry an important message. One child in the book said it best: "All the children of the world should have the chance to study."

Think Link

1. What was Tanya Roberts-Davis's purpose for writing the book *We Need to Go to School?*

2. How does the caption on this page add to your understanding of the Rugmark organization?

3. How has going to school changed life for these former child laborers?

Try It!

As you work on your investigation, think about how you can use captions for your final presentation.

Read the article to find the meanings of these words, which are also in "Lemons and Lemonade":

+ **stack**
+ **competition**
+ **expenses**
+ **demand**
+ **profit**
+ **supply**
+ **product**
+ **balance**

Vocabulary Strategy

Apposition is when a word or group of words define another word in the same sentence. Use apposition to find the meaning of *expenses*.

Vocabulary

Warm-Up

Suki gently removed one bright-red apple from the top of the stack. Max always had the produce displayed so neatly. He ran a fruit stand near the public pool.

"Just one apple today?" Max asked. "You're not giving your business to the competition are you?"

Suki smiled and shook her head. "No, Max. You know I'm a loyal customer. I'm just trying to reduce my expenses, or the money I spend to run my business. There hasn't been much demand for baby-sitters this month. My income is down."

"I guess it's tough for baby-sitters to make any profit with families away on summer vacation," Max replied. He

lifted a large box to the table and cut it open. A fresh supply of grapes had just come in.

Max thought a minute. "How would you like to help me out here?" he asked. "I was thinking it's time I expand my staff."

"Do you really mean it?" Suki asked. "I've never had a job like this."

"Well, you're one of my best customers—you sure know the product! You'll be a big help to shoppers. It's peak fruit season too. I could use an extra set of hands to help wash and set out the fruit."

"Thanks for the offer, Max. What if I get called to baby-sit? I don't want to lose that business," said Suki.

"Don't worry," Max assured her. "It'll be easy to balance your work schedules."

"Great!" exclaimed Suki. "Now, where are we going to put these grapes?"

GAME

Synonyms

List the vocabulary words on a sheet of paper. Beside each word, write a synonym for that word. When you and a classmate are both finished, compare the synonyms you listed for each vocabulary word.

Concept Vocabulary

The concept word for this lesson is **benefit.** A **benefit** is something that is helpful or that is good for a person. What are some possible benefits of having your own business? What are some possible benefits of working for someone else?

Genre

Narrative Nonfiction blends elements of fiction with elements of nonfiction to make a more exciting story. Facts about real people, places, and events are included in narrative nonfiction.

Comprehension Skill

 Fact and Opinion

As you read, identify facts and opinions within the selection.

Lemons and Lemonade

A Book about Supply and Demand

by Nancy Loewen
illustrated by Brian Jensen

Super Refreshing
MONADE
50¢

Focus Questions

What are the rewards of running your own business? What are the risks? How does supply and demand affect what you buy?

It was the third week of summer vacation, and Karly was bored, hot, and thirsty. Really thirsty. A tall glass of lemonade would really hit the spot.

"That's it!" she exclaimed. "I'll open a lemonade stand! I'll be rich!"

25¢

LEMONADE

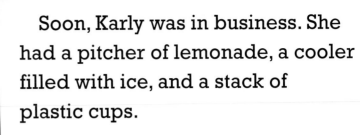

Soon, Karly was in business. She had a pitcher of lemonade, a cooler filled with ice, and a stack of plastic cups.

"All of your supplies are called capital," Mom said. "Capital is the money or goods you use to start and run a business."

Businesses can be very small, with just one person. Or they can be huge, with thousands of people all over the world.

Karly's first customer was Mrs. Crane from next door. "Mmmmm, delicious, dear," she said.

Next came the boy who mowed Mr. Smith's lawn. He was so thirsty he bought two lemonades.

Josh and Shaun, brothers from across the street, sat with Karly for a while. Together they sold lemonade to a woman out for a jog, a couple of kids on bikes, and a babysitter pulling a toddler in a wagon.

Some businesses sell goods, such as food, tires, or clothing. Others sell services, such as cutting hair or fixing cars.

At suppertime, Karly ran into the house. "Look at all this money!" she said.

Mom smiled. "You did great. That money is called your gross profit."

"Gross?" said Karly. "I don't think so!"

"Gross just means total," Mom explained. "But remember, out of that money you still need to pay for the cost of the lemonade, cups, and ice. Those are your expenses."

"Well, I'll bet there will be some money left," Karly said.

"The money you have left is called your net profit," Mom said.

Gross and net are important business terms. Gross profit, minus expenses, equals net profit.

The word "market" can mean different things. It can be a place where goods are bought and sold. But it can also refer to the people who make spending decisions.

That night, Karly made a new sign.

"I see you've raised your price," Mom noted. "You're testing the market—seeing how much people are willing to pay."

"Exactly," said Karly. "I can't wait for tomorrow!"

Karly set up her lemonade stand early the next day. A garage sale was going on down the street, and people were everywhere. Business was fantastic! Karly was completely sold out by early afternoon.

"When people want what you're selling, that's called demand," Mom explained.

"Can we go to the store and buy lots more lemonade?" Karly begged. "I don't want to run out again tomorrow."

If demand for a product is high, and not enough of that product can be made, the result is scarcity. The product is hard to find and often expensive.

In business, supply and demand are the two key factors in determining price.

The next morning was cool and windy. The garage sale was over. Hardly anyone was around, and those who were didn't want cold lemonade.

"There's no demand today," Karly complained to Mom.

"Nope," Mom said. "It's tough to balance the supply of a product with the demand for it."

Karly nodded. She decided to close up shop. She wanted a break from the lemonade business.

On the next hot day, Karly set up her lemonade stand again. No sooner had she put out her sign when she saw Josh and Shaun across the street. They had set up their own stand! All of Karly's regular customers were there.

Mom brought Karly a fruit snack. "I guess you don't have a monopoly anymore," she said.

"This isn't a game, Mom."

"I mean, your business isn't the only one anymore," Mom said. "You have competition. People have more choices."

Karly opened her fruit snack—and had a great idea.

"Be right back!" she said, as she ran into the house.

Because a monopoly has no competition, it can set prices high. But if there's competition, prices will usually be lower.

Karly returned with a bowl of fruit snacks and a new sign.

"You've cut your lemonade price to be more competitive. And by offering a new product, you've expanded your business. Nice going!" Mom said.

Business started picking up. Karly felt proud when she looked at the coins in her basket.

When businesses discount their products, they make less profit per item. But they hope to sell more of the product and make more money overall.

Fantastic Fruit Snacks 50¢

Karly's Best Ever LEMONADE

Now Just 25¢

Later that afternoon, Karly was surprised to see Josh and Shaun walking toward her.

"We were wondering if you'd like to be business partners," Josh said.

"We have this friend who lives across the street from the park," Shaun added. "There's a softball game going on today. Maybe we could go there together."

Karly thought about all the thirsty, hungry people at the park. It would be fun to work with her friends, too.

"Great idea!" she exclaimed. "Let's do it. We'll be rich!"

Meet the Author

Nancy Loewen

Nancy Loewen enjoys writing about the practical things in life. She has written over forty books, including books about money, foods from around the world, bugs, and staying safe at home and at school. Loewen lives in Minnesota.

Meet the Illustrator

Brian Jensen

Brian Jensen has worked as an artist for over twenty years. Besides making pictures for books, Jensen has also made artwork for companies. He likes to paint pictures of lakes and towns near his home. Jensen lives in Waconia, Minnesota.

Theme Connections

Within the Selection

1. How is the competition good for Karly's business? How is it bad?

2. How is the competition good for customers?

Across Selections

3. What does Karly have in common with the early traders you read about in "It's a Deal!"?

4. How are Karly's customers different from the early traders?

Beyond the Selection

5. Other than the products, what keeps customers coming back to a business?

6. What businesses other than a lemonade stand are affected by cold or rainy weather?

Write about It!

Write a list of things you might say to customers if you had your own lemonade stand.

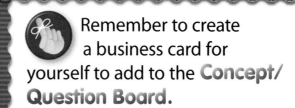

Remember to create a business card for yourself to add to the **Concept/Question Board.**

Hooray for Hybrids

Sales of hybrid cars are on the rise. What is the appeal of these gas-electric cars? Here is what hybrid owner James Wallis had to say.

Q: How is a hybrid car different from a normal car?

A: A hybrid is powered by electric as well as gas. So, it does not use as much gas as a normal car. Hybrid cars are also much quieter.

Q: What factors did you think about when choosing a car?

A: I considered the cost. Although my hybrid cost about five thousand dollars more than a normal car, I am spending less on gas now.

Also, I am glad to be less dependent on gas. In the 1970s, events in the Middle East led to an oil shortage here. The price of gas soared because of the high demand and short supply.

When hurricanes hit the U.S. in 2005, gas production slowed down and oil was scarce. This caused high prices at the pumps.

Q: Is a hybrid worth the higher cost?

A: Absolutely! I like that my hybrid causes less pollution than standard cars do. I also like that one gallon of gas takes me a lot farther!

Hybrid Car Sales in the U.S. from 2000 to 2005

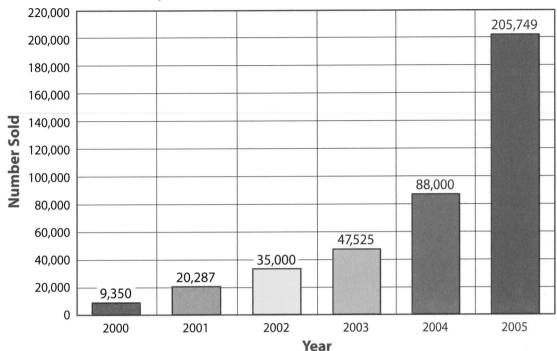

Number Sold (y-axis): 0, 20,000, 40,000, 60,000, 80,000, 100,000, 120,000, 140,000, 160,000, 180,000, 200,000, 220,000

Year (x-axis): 2000, 2001, 2002, 2003, 2004, 2005

- 2000: 9,350
- 2001: 20,287
- 2002: 35,000
- 2003: 47,525
- 2004: 88,000
- 2005: 205,749

Think Link

1. Identify three differences between hybrid cars and regular cars.

2. Why are owners of hybrid cars less affected by oil shortages?

3. Look at the bar graph. What can you predict about hybrid car sales for the next few years?

Hybrid cars like this one were first sold in the United States in 1999.

Try It!

As you work on your investigation, think about how you can use a bar graph to show your facts.

Read the article to find the meanings of these words, which are also in "Madam C. J. Walker: Self-Made Millionaire":

- ✦ wealth
- ✦ millionaire
- ✦ factory
- ✦ charged
- ✦ sued
- ✦ managed
- ✦ hired
- ✦ secretary

Vocabulary Strategy

Word Structure is when parts of a word help you understand the word's meaning. Use word structure to find the meaning of *millionaire*.

Vocabulary
Warm-Up

Have you seen ads that promise great wealth for little effort? "Get rich quick" schemes that say you can become a millionaire in no time? Many people have been tricked by them.

One common scam, "Work at home" jobs, targets people who are not able to work in a factory or office. The companies creating these ads charged a lot of money for supplies to do the work. The people who believed these ads made little or no profit. Some even lost money.

The Federal Trade Commission (FTC) is a group that puts a stop to such scams. The FTC began its work in 1914. Since then, it has helped a lot

of people. It warned people about unfair and fake offers. It sued many companies that tried to cheat people.

A group of five commissioners managed the FTC when it began. The FTC commission hired a huge team of lawyers to protect consumers. The lawyers looked into complaints that were filed. They also banned many ads making false claims.

Currently, not all FTC staff are lawyers. The group hires students too. They file, type, and do other office work. It is a great way to train for a job as a secretary. Some students go on to get law degrees.

If a deal sounds too good to be true, it probably is. Few people can get rich without a lot of hard work. Do not fall for scams that tell you otherwise.

GAME

Making Sentences

Work with a partner to create sentences using the vocabulary words. Choose two words from the list, and challenge your partner to make up a sentence using the two words. Then switch roles. Continue until all of the vocabulary words have been used.

Concept Vocabulary

The concept word for this lesson is **consumer.** A **consumer** is a person who uses goods and services. Many companies do consumer research. What kind of information do you think businesses look for? What do successful businesses know about their consumers?

Genre

A **biography** is the story of a real person's life that is written by another person.

Comprehension Strategy

Visualizing As you read, form pictures in your mind of the setting, characters, and actions in the selection.

Focus Questions

If you were to open your own business, what type of product or service would you sell? In what ways can you use your time or money to help others?

Madam C.J. Walker

Self-Made Millionaire

by Patricia and Fredrick McKissack

BLACK HERITAGE

32 USA

Madam C.J. Walker

1998

Sarah Breedlove was born in Louisiana. She was the first person in her family to be born free. As a child, Sarah did not go to school. She worked with her family on a cotton farm.

Sarah got married when she was fourteen years old. After her husband died six years later, she and her daughter, A'Lelia, moved to St. Louis, Missouri. They lived with Sarah's brothers. For eighteen years, Sarah cooked and washed clothes so A'Lelia could go to college. Sarah was then able to attend night school.

Around this time, Sarah began losing her hair. She found a job selling products which seemed to help her hair. Sarah became a successful saleswoman.

Sarah wanted to make her own hair products, however. She mixed different natural ingredients. After many hours of mixing, she found the perfect blends. In 1906, Sarah married Charles J. Walker. She started calling herself Madam C. J. Walker. She used her new name for her hair care products.

In 1908, Madam Walker opened a beauty school in Pittsburgh, Pennsylvania. Her school and company gave many African-American women their first jobs.

Madam C. J. Walker
December 23, 1867–
May 25, 1919

318

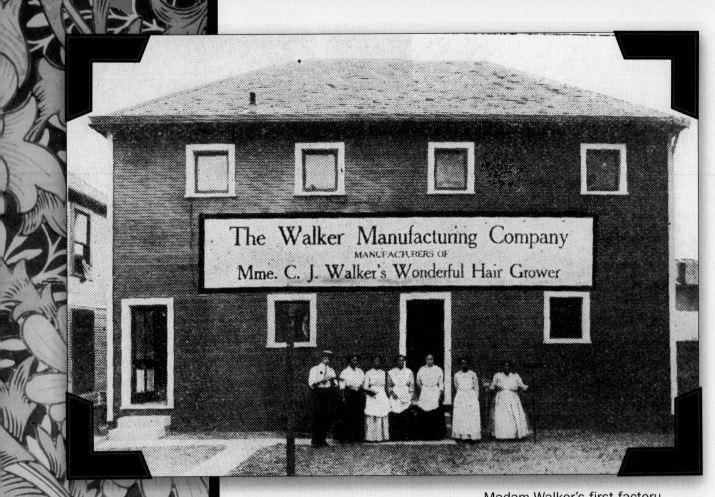
Madam Walker's first factory

In 1910, Madam Walker decided to build her first factory in Indianapolis, Indiana. Right away Madam Walker hired people to help build a strong business. Two lawyers, Robert Lee Brokenburr and Freeman Briley Ransom, managed the company.

Violet Davis Reynolds was Madam Walker's secretary and good friend. They traveled together. They showed other black women that they could start businesses, too.

Black women loved the idea! In 1910, most black women made from $2 to $10 a week. Madam Walker's hair culturists were making $20 a week or more.

Madam Walker's original product

A year after moving to Indianapolis, the company had 950 salespeople. The company earned $1,000 a month. Madam Walker put the money back into the business. By 1918, her company was earning about $250,000 a year. Madam Walker made history by becoming America's first female self-made millionaire—white or black!

Madam Walker owned several of the latest cars, such as this Model T Ford.

Other products made by the Walker company

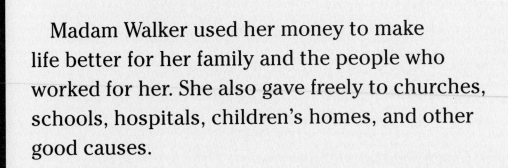

Madam Walker used her money to make life better for her family and the people who worked for her. She also gave freely to churches, schools, hospitals, children's homes, and other good causes.

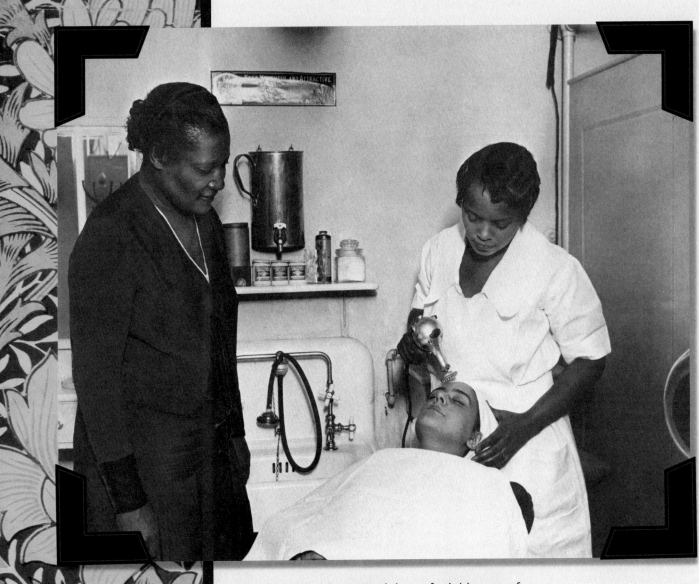

A'Lelia Walker is supervising a facial in one of Madam C. J. Walker's many beauty parlors.

Madam Walker and A'Lelia were always interested in civil rights. At that time the country was segregated. This meant that laws kept black people and white people apart. Blacks and whites couldn't ride buses or trains together. They couldn't go to the same schools.

Once Madam Walker went to a white theater. They charged her more money because she was black. First she sued the theater. Then she built the Walker building, a block-long business center in downtown Indianapolis. Inside, there was a new movie theater where black and white people could sit together.

Madam Walker helped organize a parade in 1917 to protest violence against African Americans.

A'Lelia Walker

Most jobs weren't open to blacks. Madam Walker spoke to groups all over the country. She believed black people needed to start more businesses in their own neighborhoods. Then there would be more jobs for other African Americans.

In 1913, A'Lelia moved to Harlem, a mostly black neighborhood in New York City. She wanted her mother to move the business there. Harlem was becoming the center of black life.

Walker agents gather at Villa Lewaro, Madam Walker's mansion overlooking the Hudson River in New York.

Finally Madam Walker agreed that New York was the place to live. In 1916, she left Indianapolis. But the Walker Factory stayed there. F. B. Ransom and Alice Kelly were left in charge. Alice Kelly knew Madam Walker's secret formula. Madam Walker and A'Lelia were the only other people who knew the formula at that time.

Walker in a quiet moment in her New York mansion

Madam Walker had worked hard all her life. Now her health was poor. Her doctors warned her to slow down, but she did not know how to rest. Madam Walker traveled around the country giving speeches and opening new beauty shops.

Sarah Breedlove Walker, known as Madam C. J. Walker, died on May 25, 1919. She was fifty-one years old. A'Lelia stayed in New York. She used her great wealth to help struggling black authors, artists, and musicians in the 1920s. In 1931, she died at age forty-six.

Madam Walker donated money for Indianapolis's new black YMCA. Next to her is Booker T. Washington. Behind her is F. B. Ransom.

Meet the Authors

Patricia McKissack and Fredrick McKissack

Patricia and Fredrick McKissack have been friends since childhood and married after college. As a writing team, they have written over one hundred books. Fredrick does the research for books about African-American history. Patricia focuses on the writing process. This is very different from their first careers: he was an engineer and construction worker, and she was a teacher. The McKissacks live in Missouri but spend a lot of time traveling and doing research for their books.

Money

Theme Connections

Within the Selection

1. Who do you admire for being successful in his or her job?

2. What qualities make this person good at the job?

Across Selections

3. How did Karly from "Lemons and Lemonade" and Madam C. J. Walker make their businesses grow?

4. How were secret formulas important in both "The Go-Around Dollar" and "Madam C. J. Walker"?

Beyond the Selection

5. Why are so many businesses that sell health and beauty products successful?

6. How does a strong, profitable company benefit workers in the surrounding community?

Write about It!

Explain how you would use your money to help others if you were as wealthy as Madam Walker.

Remember to cut out advertisements for health and beauty products to add to the **Concept/Question Board.**

An International Request

Dear Sir or Madam:

Last year I had the pleasure of traveling to London. While I was there, I purchased a tube of your "Soft as Velvet" hand cream. I love the product and would like to buy more. I am sorry to say that I have not been able to find the cream at any shops here in the U.S. Please let me know if it is available here. If so, at what retail stores may I find it?

Thank you for your time. I look forward to your response.

Sincerely,
Charlotte Roe

328

Dear Ms. Roe:

Thank you for inquiring about our product. We are pleased to let you know that "Soft as Velvet" hand cream will soon be produced and sold in your local area and in other states in the U.S. Each factory will release the first shipments by spring.

You might wish to try our skin- and hair-care products as well. We offer them in the same fresh fragrance as our hand cream.

Please look for our products in any fine department store. For a complete list of retail outlets, please visit our Web site.

Thank you for your interest. We hope you will continue to be a valued customer.

With best wishes,
Marley Scott, Director of Marketing

Think Link

1. Why do some customers prefer to buy a product in person instead of ordering it through the mail?

2. Why was the response addressed to "Ms. Roe" instead of "Charlotte"?

3. How does Marley Scott encourage the customer to spend more money on her company's products?

Try It!

As you work on your investigation, think of someone to whom you could write a formal business letter to request information.

Genre

Historical Fiction is a type of realistic story that is set in some specific point of the past.

Comprehension Strategy

⭐ **Adjusting Reading Speed**
As you read, you may find that some sentences are harder to read than others. Slow down or reread sentences you do not understand.

UNCLE JED'S BARBERSHOP

by Margaree King Mitchell
illustrated by James Ransome

Focus Questions
What is it like to save for a long time for something you really want? How would you feel if you saved a lot of money for something you wanted and then had to spend it on something else?

Read the article to find the meanings of these words, which are also in "Uncle Jed's Barbershop":

✦ county
✦ equipment
✦ segregation
✦ bundled
✦ stations
✦ failing
✦ unconscious

Vocabulary Strategy

Word Structure is when parts of a word help you understand the word's meaning. Use word structure to find the meaning of *unconscious*.

Vocabulary
Warm-Up

Many schools raise money to help people in need. One school worked to help people in a nearby county that had suffered damage from a storm. Other schools raise money to help people far away. There are many ways to earn funds.

Get active! Round up some sports equipment, and sell tickets to a student-teacher game. An exchange of ideas with other people is also important.

Have a "go-without" month. Make a list of things you would really miss. Would you miss TV or dessert? Examine your list closely. Make sure you have thought of things that mean a lot to you. Get sponsors to pay you for each day you give up your favorite things.

Do you feel there is segregation of age groups in your town? Bring citizens of all ages together! In the spring, help older people plant flowers. In the fall, offer to rake leaves. One winter, some friends bundled up and shoveled snow in an entire neighborhood.

Ask whether you can set up recycling stations at your school. Have a place to collect things like paper and cans. Then turn them in for money.

If you have a failing fundraiser, do not be disappointed. You never know when a good idea will come—maybe even when you are unconscious. If a good thought does come to you in a dream, make the dream come true!

GAME

Definition Game

In a small group, play a game to review the meaning of each vocabulary word. The first player might say, "What word means 'not working'?" The classmate who correctly names the word *(failing)* chooses the next definition to give to the group. Play until all of the words have been used.

Concept Vocabulary

The concept word for this lesson is *savings.* **Savings** is money saved, or set aside, for use in the future. Saving money can be difficult. Talk about why people might have savings. Why might savings be important?

Genre

Historical Fiction is a type of realistic story that is set in some specific period of the past.

Comprehension Strategy

Adjusting Reading Speed

As you read, you may find that some sentences are harder to read than others. Slow down or reread sections you do not understand.

UNCLE JED'S BARBERSHOP

by Margaree King Mitchell
illustrated by James Ransome

Focus Questions

What is it like to save for a long time for something you really want? How would you feel if you saved a lot of money for something you wanted and then had to spend it on something else?

Jedediah Johnson was my granddaddy's brother. Everybody has their favorite relative. Well, Uncle Jedediah was mine.

He used to come by our house every Wednesday night with his clippers. He was the only black barber in the county. Daddy said that before Uncle Jed started cutting hair, he and Granddaddy used to have to go thirty miles to get a haircut.

After Uncle Jed cut my daddy's hair, he lathered a short brush with soap and spread it over my daddy's face and shaved him. Then he started over on my granddaddy.

I always asked Uncle Jed to cut my hair, but Mama wouldn't let him. So he would run the clippers on the back of my neck and just pretend to cut my hair. He even spread lotion on my neck. I would smell wonderful all day.

When he was done, he would pick me up and sit me in his lap and tell me about the barbershop he was going to open one day and about all the fancy equipment that would be in it. The sinks would be so shiny they sparkled, the floors so clean you could see yourself. He was going to have four barber chairs. And outside was going to be a big, tall, red-and-white barber pole. He told me he was saving up for it.

He had been saying the same things for years. Nobody believed him. People didn't have dreams like that in those days.

We lived in the South. Most people were poor. My daddy owned a few acres of land and so did a few others. But most people were sharecroppers. That meant they lived in a shack and worked somebody else's land in exchange for a share of the crop.

When I was five years old, I got sick. This particular morning, I didn't come into the kitchen while Mama was fixing breakfast. Mama and Daddy couldn't wake me up. My nightgown and the bedclothes were all wet where I had sweated.

Mama wrapped me in a blanket while Daddy went outside and hitched the horse to the wagon. We had to travel about twenty miles into town to the hospital. It was midday when we got there. We had to go to the colored waiting room. In those days, they kept blacks and whites separate. There were separate public rest rooms, separate water fountains, separate schools. It was called segregation. So in the hospital, we had to go to the colored waiting room.

Even though I was unconscious, the doctors wouldn't look at me until they had finished with all the white patients. When the doctors did examine me, they told my daddy that I needed an operation and that it would cost three hundred dollars.

Three hundred dollars was a lot of money in those days. My daddy didn't have that kind of money. And the doctors wouldn't do the operation until they had the money.

My mama bundled me back up in the blanket and they took me home. Mama held me in her arms all night. She kept me alive until Daddy found Uncle Jed. He found him early the next morning in the next county on his way to cut somebody's hair. Daddy told him about me.

Uncle Jed leaned on his bent cane and stared straight ahead. He told Daddy that the money didn't matter. He couldn't let anything happen to his Sarah Jean.

Well, I had the operation. For a long time after that, Uncle Jed came by the house every day to see how I was doing. I know that three hundred dollars delayed him from opening the barbershop.

Uncle Jed came awfully close to opening his shop a few years after my operation. He had saved enough money to buy the land and build the building. But he still needed money for the equipment.

Anyway, Uncle Jed had come by the
house. We had just finished supper when
there was a knock on the door. It was Mr.
Ernest Walters, a friend of Uncle Jed's.
He had come by to tell Uncle Jed about
the bank failing. That was where Mr.
Walters and Uncle Jed had their money.
Uncle Jed had over three thousand
dollars in the bank, and it was gone.

Uncle Jed just stood there a long time
before he said anything. Then he told
Mr. Walters that even though he was
disappointed, he would just have to start
all over again.

Talk about some hard times. That was the beginning of the Great Depression. Nobody had much money.

But Uncle Jed kept going around to his customers cutting their hair, even though they couldn't pay him. His customers shared with him whatever they had—a hot meal, fresh eggs, vegetables from the garden. And when they were able to pay again, they did.

And Uncle Jed started saving all over again.

Ol' Uncle Jed finally got his barbershop. He opened it on his seventy-ninth birthday. It had everything, just like he said it would—big comfortable chairs, four cutting stations. You name it! The floors were so clean, they sparkled.

On opening day, people came from all over the county. They were Ol' Uncle Jed's customers. He had walked to see them for so many years. That day they all came to him.

I believe he cut hair all night and all the next day and the next night and the day after that! That man was so glad to have that shop, he didn't need any sleep.

Of course, I was there, too. I wouldn't have missed it for the world. When I sat in one of the big barber chairs, Uncle Jed patted the back of my neck with lotion like he always did. Then he twirled me round and round in the barber chair.

Uncle Jed died not long after that, and I think he died a happy man. You see, he made his dream come true even when nobody else believed in it.

He taught me to dream, too.

Meet the Author

Margaree King Mitchell

Margaree King Mitchell was inspired to become a children's book writer while volunteering in her son's classroom. She decided to help "inspire children to achieve their dreams." She wanted to teach students the importance of having dreams and staying in school. Mitchell also writes television scripts and plays.

Meet the Illustrator

James Ransome

James Ransome loved to look at the illustrations in comic books as a child. Now that he is an illustrator, he wants his characters to look real. To get ideas for one picture, Ransom may take dozens of photographs of a person and background. Then he creates a beautiful picture with many realistic details.

Theme Connections

Within the Selection

1. How would you feel if someone gave up his or her savings to help you?

2. How would it feel to be able to help someone else in that way?

Across Selections

3. How is Madam Walker from the previous selection like Uncle Jed in this selection?

4. How are they different?

Beyond the Selection

5. Are relationships with friends and family more important than money? Explain.

6. How does a person's attitude affect his or her ability to succeed in business?

Write about It!

Describe the career you would like to have as an adult.

Remember to cut out words that you think represent things that money cannot buy to add to the **Concept/Question Board**.

Genre

Expository Text tells readers something. It contains facts about real people or events.

Feature

Headings tell readers what a paragraph is going to be about.

THE GREAT DEPRESSION

The Great Depression was a bleak time. Many people lost their jobs and homes. With banks failing, families lost all of their savings. People asked, "How could this happen?"

THE OLDEST FORM OF TRADE

The exchange of goods became the way to get some needed goods. A car might be exchanged for a cow. Someone might trade coffee for a pot or pan.

LINES FOR FOOD

Cupboards once filled with food were now bare. Soup kitchens served hungry people a warm meal. Many stood in line for hours to get a bit of free food.

SEARCHING FOR HOMES

Many people could no longer pay for their homes. They had to search for new places to live. Some were able to move in with relatives. Others were not so lucky. They lived in their cars or shacks built from scraps.

HARD TIMES HERE AND THERE

Some people went to Cleveland and Detroit to look for work. The car industry was big in these cities. However car sales were dropping, so more jobs were lost. Even workers in Asia suffered. Car makers had bought rubber and tin from Asia. Now money to buy such goods was gone.

HOPE AND HEALING

In 1932 Americans chose a new president, Franklin Roosevelt. He pledged to put people back to work and to help the nation's poor. This was part of his New Deal plan. Thanks to this plan, the country pulled through its hard times.

Think Link

1. How is the heading for the third paragraph helpful?

2. How did America's Great Depression affect people in other parts of the world?

3. People who lost their homes and moved in with relatives were considered lucky. Explain why.

Try It!

As you work on your investigation, think about what paragraph headings you could use when planning your final presentation.

347

Focus Questions Does a business always mean a lot of work? When can it be fun to be in business?

Lemonade Stand

by Myra Cohn Livingston

illustrated by Laura Freeman-Hines

Every summer
under the shade
we fix up a stand
to sell lemonade.

A stack of cups,
a pitcher of ice,
a shirtboard sign
to tell the price.

A dime for the big,
A nickel for small.
The nickel cup's short.
The dime cup's tall.

Plenty of sugar
to make it sweet,
and sometimes cookies
for us to eat.

But when the sun
moves into the shade
it gets too hot
to sell lemonade.

Nobody stops
so we put things away
and drink what's left
and start to play.

349

TONY and the QUARTER

by Jack Prelutsky
illustrated by Erica Pelton Villnave

Tony's my neighbor
and Tony's my friend.
Today Tony's ma
gave him money to spend.

He slapped my behind
and he said with a laugh,
"Whatever I get,
you can have almost half.

I got a whole quarter,
I'll split it with you.
Let's go get some candy
and bubble gum too."

So happily downhill
the two of us tore,
to see what a quarter
would buy at the store.

But things didn't work
just the way that we planned,
Tony tripped—and the quarter
flew out of his hand.

It rolled down the sidewalk
and oh, what a pain!
We couldn't catch up
and it went down the drain.

Such a dumb thing to do,
oh, it made me so sore.
Still, I guess I like Tony
as much as before.

Unit 3

Test Prep

Test-Taking Strategy: Comparing Answer Choices

Be sure to look at all the answers to a question. Compare the answers to one another. Choose the answer you think is best.

Comparing Answer Choices

Look carefully at every answer when you take a test. It is easy to skip an answer choice or to misunderstand what it means. Also, think about what the question is asking.

> **Read the sentences. What does the word *dreadful* mean? Read the answer choices and decide which answer is best.**
>
> The weather was *dreadful*. It was cold, rainy, and windy.
> Ⓐ pleasant   Ⓑ changing
> Ⓒ terrible   Ⓓ snowy

Think about the sentences. They say that the weather was cold, rainy, and windy. Look at the answer choices. All of the answers tell about weather. Only one answer tells about cold, rainy, and windy weather. The word *terrible* best describes this kind of weather.

Terrible is the answer because it means about the same as *dreadful*. It is better than the other answers and makes sense with the information in the sentences.

352

Test-Taking Practice

Read the story "An Expensive Day." Then answer numbers 1 through 4.

On the way to the theme park, the three children talked about their favorite rides.

Jen asked, "Are we staying at the hotel with the big pool?"

Mother said it was too expensive. They were only going to spend one day at the park. They would drive home that night.

"What does expensive mean?" asked Maria, the youngest child.

"That's when something costs more than we want to spend," said Mother. "We want to have money for other things at the park, like food and rides."

Juan, the oldest brother, asked how much it cost to go inside the park. Father said that tickets cost $30.00 for each adult and $15.00 for each of the three children.

"No way," said Juan. He and the other children could not believe that it cost that much money to visit the theme park.

"There's more," added Father. "Each ride will cost $2.00."

The children asked how many rides they could go on. Father said they planned enough money for five rides for each child. Maria wanted to know if she could buy some cotton candy and caramel corn. Mother said that they could each have one food treat. Each treat would cost around $4.00.

Later that day, the three children asked if they could go to the theme park gift shop. The toys that they liked cost $5.00 each. Mother said they could each get one gift. She said they had to make a choice. They could keep the souvenir or give it to a friend.

On the way home from the park, Father stopped for gas. It cost almost $50.00 to fill the gas tank. Juan scribbled some numbers on a pad and was shocked. He told his family that they spent over $200.00 at the park that day.

"Wow," said Jen. "That's a lot of money. Thank you for saving enough to take us to the park."

Use what you learned from "An Expensive Day" to answer Numbers 1 through 4. Write your answers on a piece of paper.

Test Tips

- Think about the question.

- Say the question to yourself.

- Choose the best answer to the question.

1. What did Juan scribble on a pad?

Ⓐ The names of the roads they drove on

Ⓑ All the other vacations they have had

Ⓒ The name of each ride at the park

Ⓓ All the money they spent that day

2. What happens before the family reaches the park?

Ⓐ Father explains how many rides each child can go on.

Ⓑ The children buy something at the gift shop.

Ⓒ Juan adds up how much money they will spend.

Ⓓ Maria buys cotton candy and caramel corn.

3. Juan is shocked at the end of the story because

Ⓐ the hotel with the big pool is too expensive.

Ⓑ his sisters decide to give gifts to their friends.

Ⓒ his parents spent so much money during the day.

Ⓓ it takes so long to drive home from the park.

4. Why does the author say how much everything costs at the theme park?

Ⓐ To warn the reader against spending money

Ⓑ To show how expensive everything is

Ⓒ To explain where the family was going

Ⓓ To explain what a theme park is

355

Pronunciation Key

a as in **a**t
ā as in l**a**te
â as in c**a**re
ä as in f**a**ther
e as in s**e**t
ē as in m**e**
i as in **i**t
ī as in k**i**te
o as in **o**x
ō as in r**o**se

ô as in b**ou**ght and r**a**w
oi as in c**oi**n
o͝o as in b**oo**k
o͞o as in t**oo**
or as in f**or**m
ou as in **ou**t
u as in **u**p
ū as in **u**se
ûr as in t**ur**n, g**er**m, l**ear**n, f**ir**m, w**or**k

ə as in **a**bout, chick**e**n, penc**i**l, cann**o**n, circ**u**s
ch as in **ch**air
hw as in w**h**ich
ng as in ri**ng**
sh as in **sh**op
th as in **th**in
t͟h as in **th**ere
zh as in trea**s**ure

The mark (ˊ) is placed after a syllable with a heavy accent, as in **chicken** (**chik**ˊ ən).

The mark (ˋ) after a syllable shows a lighter accent, as in **disappear** (**dis**ˊ əp pērˊ).

Glossary

A

aboard (ə bôrd´) *prep.* On or into a ship, train, or an airplane.

actually (ak´ shū əl lē´) *adv.* In fact; really.

adopt (əd opt´) *n.* To take and use as one's own.

affection (əf fek´ shən) *n.* A friendly feeling of liking or loving.

ancient (ān´ shənt) *adj.* Very old.

announced (ən nouns´ d) *v.* Past tense of **announce:** To make known.

apathetic (ap´ əth et´ ic) *adj.* Having or showing little interest, concern, or desire to act.

appointed (əp point´ əd) *v.* A form of the verb **appoint:** To name for an office.

appreciate (əp prē´ shē āt´) *v.* To understand the value of.

assure (əsh ûr´) *n.* To make certain or sure.

astonished (əs ton´ ish d) *adj.* Greatly surprised.

B

bacteria (bak tē´ rēə) *n.* Plural form of **bacterium:** A tiny living cell that can be seen only through a microscope. Some cause disease; others help, such as making soil richer.

bacteria

balance (bal´ əns) *adv.* To make equal in weight, amount, or force. *n.* A steady, secure position.

barber (bär´ bûr) *n.* A person whose work is cutting hair, and shaving and trimming beards.

357

Pronunciation Key: at; lāte; câre; fäther; set; mē; it; kīte; ox; rōse; ô in bought; coin; bŏŏk; tōō; form; out; up; ūse; tûrn; ə sound in about, chicken, pencil, cannon, circus; chair; hw in which; ring; shop; thin; there; zh in treasure.

bargain (bär´ gən) *n.* An agreement to trade.

barter (bär´ dûr) *n.* The trade of one thing for another without using money.

beckoned (bek´ ən d) *v.* Past tense of **beckon:** To call someone by waving.

benefit (ben´ ə fit) *n.* Something that helps or that is good for a person.

blooming (blōōm ing) *v.* A form of the verb **bloom:** To flower; to blossom.

boards (bordz) *n.* Plural form of **board:** A long, flat piece of sawed wood.

bore (bōr) *v.* To make a hole by digging or drilling.

bother (both´ ûr) *v.* To annoy.

break (brāk) *n.* A short rest period.

brightened (brīt´ ən d) *v.* Past tense of **brighten:** To light up.

bringing up (bring´ ing up) *n.* Raising, as in children.

bundled (bun´ dəl d) *v.* Past tense of **bundle:** To wrap together.

C

causes (koz´ əz) *n.* Plural form of **cause:** Something a person or group believes in.

cautiously (kosh´ əs lē´) *adv.* With close care.

certain (sûr´ tən) *adj.* Sure.

challenge (chal´ lənj) *n.* To question the truth of.

charged (chärj´ d) *v.* Past tense of **charge:** To ask a price.

chores (chorz) *n.* Plural form of **chore:** A small job.

chores

city limits (sit´ ē lim´ its) *n.* The points at which the city ends.

civil rights (siv´ əl rīts´) *n.* Plural form of **civil right:** The rights of every citizen of a country, including the right to vote and the right to equal protection under the law.

clung (klung) *v.* Past tense of **cling:** To stick closely.

collected (kəl lekt´ əd) *v.* A form of the verb **collect:** To gather together.

colony (kol´ ən ē) *n.* A group of animals or plants of the same kind that live together.

compete (cəm pēt´) *v.* To try to win.

competition (kom´ pət ish´ ən) *n.* The act of trying to win or gain something from another or others.

completely (kəm plēt´ lē) *adv.* Entirely.

condition (kən dish´ ən) *n.* Something needed for another event to happen.

consumer (kən sōōm´ ûr) *n.* A person who uses goods and services.

counterfeit (koun´ tûr fit´) *adj.* Fake.

county (coun´ tē) *n.* Part of a state.

cozy (cō´ zē) *adj.* Warm and comfortable.

curious (kyur´ ē əs) *adj.* Interested in knowing.

currency (kûr´ ren sē) *n.* Money—coins and paper—that people use.

customer (kus´ təm ûr´) *n.* A person who buys something at a store or uses the services of a business.

dawn (dôn) *n.* The first light that appears in the morning; daybreak.

deal (dēl) *n.* An agreement.

debts (dets) *n.* Plural form of **debt:** Something that is owed to another.

delayed (də lā´ d) *v.* Past tense of **delay:** To put off to a later time.

demand (də mand´) *n.* The desire for a product or service.

depended (də pend´ əd) *v.* Past tense of **depend:** To rely on; to trust.

deserted (də zûrt´ əd) *v.* A form of the verb **desert:** To leave alone.

design (də zīn´) *n.* A drawing made to serve as a pattern.

design

despair (də spâr´) *n.* A complete loss of hope.

detect (də tekt´) *v.* To find out.

disappointed (dis əp point´ əd) *v.* A form of the verb **disappoint:** To make someone unhappy that something expected did not occur.

dither (dith´ ûr) *n.* A confused, upset feeling.

dwellers (dwel´ ûrz) *n.* Plural form of **dweller:** A person or an animal that lives in a certain place.

E

ecosystem (ek´ ō sis´ təm) *n.* A group of living things and the environment in which they live.

emblem (em´ bləm) *n.* A sign or figure that stands for something.

energy (en´ ûr jē) *n.* The strength or eagerness to do something.

enormous (ē nor´ məs) *adj.* Very big.

enthusiastic (en tho͞o´ zē ast´ ik) *adj.* Very excited about something.

environment (en vī´ rən mənt´) *n.* The surroundings that affect living things.

equal (ē´ kwəl) *n.* Someone who is at the same level as others.

equipment (ə kwip´ mənt) *n.* Tools and supplies used for a given purpose.

especially (is pesh´ əl lē) *adv.* Particularly.

eventually (ē ven´ tū əl lē´) *adv.* Finally.

examine (egz am´ in) *v.* To look at in detail.

examine

except (igs ept´) *prep.* Only.

exchange (eks chānj´) *n.* A trade of one thing for another.

exclaimed (eks klām´ d) *v.* Past tense of **exclaim:** To speak out.

expanded (eks pand´ əd) *v.* A form of the verb **expand:** To make larger or become larger.

expenses (eks pens´ əz) *n.* Plural form of **expense:** Money spent to buy or do something; cost.

explorer (eks plor´ ûr) *n.* A person who travels in search of geographical or scientific information.

extended (eks tend´ əd) *v.* Past tense of **extend:** To reach out.

factory (fak´ tûr ē) *n.* A building or group of buildings where things are manufactured; a plant.

factory

failing (fāl´ ing) *adj.* Losing money.

faith (fāth) *n.* Belief or trust in someone's ability or goodness.

farewell (fâr wel´) *adj.* Good-bye and good luck.

female (fē´ māl) *n.* A woman or girl.

flapped (flap´ d) *v.* Past tense of **flap:** To move up and down, as in wings.

flattered (flat´ tûr d) *v.* A form of the verb **flatter:** To praise too much without meaning.

foreign (for´ ən)) *adj.* Of or from another country.

formula (for´ mū lə´) *n.* A set method for doing something.

forms (formz) *n.* Plural form of **form:** Kind; type.

freely (frē´ lē) *adv.* Without cost.

fungi (fun´ gī) *n.* Plural form of **fungus:** A large group of living things that have cell walls similar to those in plants, but that have no flowers, leaves, or green coloring. Fungi live on plant or animal matter.

G

gathered (gath´ ûr d) *v.* Past tense of **gather:** To bring together; to collect.

glum (glum) *adj.* Very unhappy or disappointed.

graduate (graj´ ū āt´) *v.* To finish at a school and be given a diploma.

graduation (graj´ ū ā shən´) *n.* Ceremony for finishing at a school.

grateful (grāt´ fəl) *adj.* Thankful.

grazed (grāz´ d) *v.* Past tense of **graze:** To feed on grass or other plants.

grief (grēf) *n.* A very great feeling of being sad.

habitats (hab´ it ats´) *n.* Plural form of **habitat:** The place where an animal or a plant naturally lives and grows.

hatch (hach) *v.* To come out of an egg.

heartbroken (härt´ brō´ kən) *adj.* Filled with sorrow or grief.

hired (hīûr d) *v.* Past tense of **hire:** To give a job to; to employ.

hitched (hich´ d) *v.* Past tense of **hitch:** To tie up with a rope, strap, or hook.

hoes (hōz) *n.* Plural form of **hoe:** A tool used to loosen soil around plants and dig up weeds.

hoe

hollow (hol´ lō) *adj.* Having a hole or an empty space inside.

honesty (ôn´əs tē) *n.* Truthfulness.

hooves (hōovz) *n.* Plural form of **hoof:** A hard covering on the feet of animals such as horses and cows.

host (hōst) *n.* A person who invites people to visit as guests.

humiliations (hū mil ē ā´ shənz) *n.* Plural form of **humiliation:** A feeling of shame or extreme embarrassment.

ignore (ig nor´) *adv.* To pay no attention to.

insisted (in sist´ əd) *v.* Past tense of **insist:** To demand or say in a strong, firm manner.

inspect (in spekt´) *v.* To look at closely.

jealous (jel´ əs) *adj.* Being angry or upset because of what a person has or can do.

kindness (kīnd´ nəs) *n.* Showing gentle and caring behavior toward others.

kingdom (king´ dəm) *n.* A country that is ruled by a king or a queen.

lawyers (lō´ ēûrz´) *n.* Plural form of **lawyer:** A person who has studied the law and can give legal advice and represent people in court.

layer (lā´ ûr) *n.* One thickness of something.

layer

Pronunciation Key: at; l**ā**te; c**â**re; f**ä**ther; s**e**t; m**ē**; **i**t; k**ī**te; **o**x; r**ō**se; **ô** in b**ou**ght; c**oi**n; b**oo**k; t**oo**; f**or**m; **ou**t; **u**p; **ū**se; t**û**rn; **ə** sound in **a**bout, chick**e**n, penc**i**l, cann**o**n, circ**u**s; **ch**air; **hw** in **wh**ich; ri**ng**; **sh**op; **th**in; **th**ere; **zh** in trea**s**ure.

leagues (lēgz) *n.* Plural form of **league:** A group of teams.

ledges (ledg´ əz) *n.* Plural form of **ledge:** A narrow shelf or surface like a shelf.

legal tender (lē´ gəl ten´ dûr) *n.* Legally valid money that may be offered in payment of a debt.

line (līn) *v.* To cover the inside of.

lotion (lō´ shən) *n.* A special liquid for the skin that heals, soothes, softens, or cleans.

magnificent (mag nif´ is ənt´) *adj.* Very beautiful and grand; splendid.

mainland (mān´ lənd) *n.* The chief landmass of a country, or continent, as different from an island.

male (māl) *adj.* Of or having to do with men or boys.

managed (man ij´ d) *v.* Past tense of **manage:** To direct or control.

marbles (mär´ bəlz) *n.* Plural form of **marble:** A small, hard ball of glass used in games.

maze (māz) *n.* A confusing series of paths or passageways through which people might get lost.

maze

meadows (med´ ōz)) *n.* Plural form of **meadow:** A field of grassy land used as a pasture for animals.

mercy (mûr sē) *n.* Kindness or forgiveness greater than what is expected or deserved.

migrating (mī grāt´ ing) *adj.* Moving from one place to another.

mild (mīld) *adj.* Gentle or calm; not harsh or sharp.

millionaire (mil´ lē ən âr´) *n.* A person who has money or property worth a million or more dollars.

miserable (miz´ ûr əbəl´) *adj.* Very unhappy.

misfortune (mis for´ chən) *n.* Bad luck.

moist (moist) *adj.* Slightly wet; damp.

molt (mōlt) *n.* To lose or shed hair, feathers, skin, or a shell.

molt

mood (mo͞od) *n.* The way a person feels at a certain time.

moped (mōp d) *v.* Past tense of **mope:** To act sad and gloomy.

N

nation (nā´ shən) *n.* A country.

nervous (nûr´ vəs) *adj.* Uneasy.

notes (nōts) *n.* Plural form of **note:** A piece of paper with a written promise to pay someone a sum of money.

O

operation (op ûr ā´ shən) *n.* Treatment on a person or an animal by surgery.

opponents (əp pō´ nəntz) *n.* Plural form of **opponent:** A person on the other side.

opportunity (op pûr to͞o´ nət ē) *n.* A good chance to do something.

opposing (əp pōz´ ing) *adj.* Against something or someone.

organizations (or´ gən ə zā´ shənz) *n.* Plural form of **organization:** A group of people joined together for a purpose.

P

pale (pâl) *adj.* Not bright in color.

partners (pärt´ nûrz) *n.* Plural form of **partner:** A person who runs a business with one or more other persons.

pastel (pas tel´) *adj.* A pale, soft shade of a color.

patch (pach) *n.* A small area.

patient (pā´ shənt) *adj.* Willing to wait.

peculiar (pik ēoō´ lē ûr´) *adj.* Not usual; strange.

peer pressure (pēr´ presh´ ûr) *n.* Peers are people who are the same age or in the same group. Peer pressure is when one or more members of the group try to influence one another in the group.

permission (pûr mish´ ən) *n.* When an adult allows one to do something.

persuaded (pûr swād´ əd) *v.* Past tense of **persuade:** To convince.

picturing (pik´ shûr ing´) *adj.* Visualizing; making a picture in one's own mind.

plains (plānz) *n.* Plural form of **plain:** An area of flat, or almost flat, land.

plains

plumpest (plump´ əst) *adj.* Fullest and roundest.

pond (pond) *n.* A small lake.

population (pop´ ū lā´ shən) *n.* The number of people or animals who live in a place.

portrait (por´ trət) *n.* A picture of someone.

possess (pəz zes´) *v.* To have; to own.

prejudice (predj´ ə dis´) *n.* Hatred or unfair treatment of a particular group, such as members of a race or religion.

presses (pres´ əz) *n.* Plural form of **press:** A printing machine.

prey (prā) *n.* An animal that is hunted by another animal for food.

product (prod´uct) *n.* Anything that is made or created.

profit (prof´it) *n.* The amount of money left after all the costs of running a business have been paid.

protect (prə tekt´) *v.* To keep something or someone safe.

proud (proud) *adj.* Having a strong sense of satisfaction in a person or thing.

provide (prō vīd´) *v.* To give what is needed or wanted.

provoke (prə vōk´) *adv.* To make angry.

pyramid (pē´rəm id´) *n.* An object that has triangular sides that meet at a point at the top.

pyramid

R

raft (raft) *n.* A kind of flat boat made of logs or boards fixed firmly together.

recognize (rek´əg nīz´) *n.* To know and remember from before; to identify.

relative (rel´ə tiv) *n.* A person who belongs to the same family as someone else.

relocates (rē´lō kāts´) *v.* A form of the verb **relocate:** To move to a new place.

remained (rē mān´d) *v.* Past tense of **remain:** To be left.

remains (rē mānz´) *v.* A form of the verb **remain:** To be left.

resist (rə zist´) *n.* To keep from giving in to.

responded (rə spônd´əd) *v.* Past tense of **respond:** To answer.

responsibility (ri spon´sə bi´li tē) *n.* A duty.

rich (rich) *adj.* Able to produce much; fertile.

ripest (rīp´əst) *adj.* The readiest to be eaten; very ripe.

roost (rōōst) *adv.* To rest or sleep as a bird does.

rule (rōōl) *v.* To have control over.

Pronunciation Key: at; l**ā**te; c**â**re; f**ä**ther; s**e**t; m**ē**; **i**t; k**ī**te; **o**x; r**ō**se; **ô** in b**o**ught; c**oi**n; b**oo**k; t**oo**; f**o**rm; **ou**t; **u**p; **ū**se; t**û**rn; **ə** sound in **a**bout, chick**e**n, penc**i**l, cann**o**n, circ**u**s; **ch**air; **hw** in **wh**ich; ri**ng**; **sh**op; **th**in; **th**ere; **zh** in trea**s**ure.

S

sacrifice (sak´ rə fīs´) *n.* Something a person gives up for the sake of someone else.

savings (sāv´ ingz´) *pl. n.* Money saved, or set aside, for use in the future.

seal (sēl) *n.* An official stamp.

secretary (sek´ rə tâ´ rē) *n.* A person whose job is to write letters and keep records for another person or a business.

segregated (seg´ rə gāt´ əd) *v.* A form of the verb **segregate:** To set apart.

segregation (se grə gā´ shən) *n.* The practice of setting one group apart from another.

serial numbers (sē´ rē əl´ num´ bûrz) *n.* Plural form of **serial number:** A number in a series used for identification.

serial numbers

series (sē´ rēz) *pl. n.* Several in a row.

settled down (set´ təl d doun´) *v.* Past tense of **settle down:** To make one's home.

several (sev´ ər əl) *adj.* More than two, but not many.

severe (səv ēr´) *adj.* Strict.

shallow (shal´ lō) *adj.* Not deep.

sharp (shärp) *adj.* Alert.

shelter (shel´ tûr) *n.* Something that covers or protects from weather or danger.

sighed (sī d) *v.* Past tense of **sigh:** To make a long, deep breathing sound because of sadness, tiredness, or relief.

splendor (splen´ dûr) *n.* A great display, as of riches or beautiful objects.

sold out (sōld out) *v.* A form of the verb **sell out:** To sell all of the items that were for sale.

solemnly (sol´ əm lē´) *adv.* Seriously.

solution (səl ū´ shən) *n.* The answer to a problem.

stack (stak) *n.* A pile.

stack

stamped (stamp´ d) *v.* Past tense of **stamp:** To mark with a tool that makes or prints a design, numbers, or letters.

stand (stand) *n.* A booth or counter where things are sold.

stations (stā shənz) *n.* Plural form of **station:** A place where a service is performed.

stored (stor´ d) *v.* A form of the verb **store:** To put away for future use.

stranded (strand´ əd) *v.* A form of the verb **strand:** To leave in a helpless position.

strange (strānj) *adj.* Unusual.

streaked (strēk d) *v.* Past tense of **streak:** To mark with long, thin marks.

struggled (strug´ gəl d) *v.* Past tense of **struggle:** To make a great effort.

sued (sū´ d) *v.* Past tense of **sue:** To start a case against in a court of law.

suffer (suf´ fûr) *v.* To have pain or sorrow.

suited (soot´ əd) *v.* Past tense of **suit:** To meet the needs of.

supply (səp plī´) *n.* A quantity of something ready to be used.

suppose (səp pōz´) *v.* To imagine being possible.

surface (sûr´ fəs) *n.* The outside of a thing.

surrounding (sûr round´ ing) *adj.* Forming a circle around.

survive (sûr vīv´) *v.* To live through; to continue to exist.

swamps (swämps) *n.* Plural form of **swamp:** An area of wet land which may have trees and shrubs growing in it.

Pronunciation Key: at; lāte; câre; fäther; **s**et; mē; **i**t; kīte; **o**x; rōse; ô in bought; coin; book; too; form; out; up; ūse; tûrn; ə sound in about, chicken, pencil, cannon, circus; chair; hw in which; ring; shop; thin; there; zh in treasure.

swarming (sworm´ ing) *adj.* Moving in a large group.

territory (ter´ rit or´ ē) *n.* Any large area of land, usually owned by someone or by a country.

thoughtfulness (thot´ fəl nəs´) *n.* Showing concern for others and their feelings.

timidly (tim´ id lē) *adv.* In a way that shows shyness or a lack of courage.

traders (trā´ dûrz) *n.* Plural form of **trader:** A person who buys and sells things as a business.

trainers (trā´ nûrz) *n.* Plural form of **trainer:** One who teaches people or animals.

trainer

translation (tranz lā´ shən) *n.* A changing of a speech or piece of writing into another language.

treated (trēt´ əd) *v.* A form of the verb **treat:** To act a certain way toward someone.

trusted (trust´ əd) *v.* Past tense of **trust:** To believe to be true, honest, or reliable.

unconscious (un kon´ shəs) *adj.* Not awake.

valuable (val´ ū bəl´) *adj.* Worth much money.

variety (vər ī´ ə tē´) *n*. A number of different things.

vast (vast) *adj*. Very great in size.

waddled (wäd´ dəl d) *v*. Past tense of **waddle:** To walk with short steps, swaying the body from side to side.

warned (worn d) *v*. Past tense of **warn:** To tell about something that may happen; put on guard.

wealth (welth) *n*. Riches.

weighs (wāz) *v*. A form of the verb **weigh:** To be of a certain heaviness.

weigh

whined (hwīn d) *v*. Past tense of **whine:** To cry in a soft, high, complaining voice.

wildlife (wīld´ līf) *n*. Living things, especially animals, in their natural environments.

worried (wûr´ rē d) *v*. A form of the verb **worry:** To think about troubles.

worth (wûrth) *prep*. Equal in value to. *n*. The money that someone is willing to pay for something.

Photo Credits